I0636667

WEDDING BELLS AND CHIMNEY SWEEPS

WEDDING BELLS AND CHIMNEY SWEEPS

BRUCE MONTAGUE

Published by John Blake Publishing Ltd,
3 Bramber Court, 2 Bramber Road,
London W14 9PB, England

www.johnblakepublishing.co.uk

www.facebook.com/Johnblakepub facebook
twitter.com/johnblakepub twitter

First published in hardback in 2014

ISBN: 978-1-78219-225-1

British Library Cataloguing-in-Publication Data:
a catalogue record for this book is available from the British Library.

Design by www.envydesign.co.uk

Printed in Great Britain by CPI Group (UK) Ltd

1 3 5 7 9 10 8 6 4 2

Papers used by John Blake Publishing are natural, recyclable products made from wood grown in sustainable forests. The manufacturing processes conform to the environmental regulations of the country of origin.

This book is dedicated to Miranda, Kit and Natasha.

When the time comes for passing on their genes, I hope this book may still have some relevance and be of interest to them.

B.M.

Contents

Prologue xv

Chapter 1

Thinking about it

The bottom drawer 18
Choosing the right month 18
Divinations and superstitions 21
St Valentine's Day 22
Bridal showers 25
The dolly bag or wedding purse (Dorothy bag) 25
The banns 25
Red tape before marriage 26
Marriage bars 28
Closed seasons for church weddings 28
The Art of Courtly Love . 29
Free love and love beads . . 30

Chapter 2

Leading up to it

Choosing the right day . . . 32
The engagement 34
Engagement rings 34
Princess Diana's engagement ring 35
Precious stones – their symbolism 36
Kneeling to propose 37
Sex manuals for the young bride 37
Church or civil? 38
The bride's list 39
The groom's list 39
Changing the surname 39
Common-law marriage . . . 40
Marriage by ships' captains 41
Las Vegas weddings 42
A short list of confusing definitions: 43
betrothal and espousal . . 43
bridezilla 43
civil marriage 43
commitment ceremony 44
domestic partnership . . . 44
Espousal 45
Mail-order bride 45
Marriage/Matrimony 46
marriage bonds 46
marriage licence 47
To plight one's troth 47
shoshbin 47
spouse 47
shotgun wedding 47
special licence 48
trousseau 50
The wedding industry 50

Chapter 3

FOREPLAY

Something old – something new 52
The show of presents 53
The wedding guest book .. 53
The best man (or groomsman) 54
The best man's checklist ... 55
The wooden spoon 56
The boutonnière 57
The thistle 57
Tuxedos 57
The marriage certificate ... 59
Marriage registers 59
Wedding favours 59
Love tokens 60
To pre-nup or not pre-nup? 60
The 'blackening' ritual 61
Marry and live longer 62
Nuns 62

Chapter 4

DOING IT

Wedding bells 66
Wedding dresses 67
World's longest wedding dresses 70
Princess Diana's wedding dress 70
The Duchess of Cambridge's wedding dress 71
Queen Victoria's wedding dress 71
Queen Elizabeth II's wedding dress 72
Floral bridal crowns 72
Wedding marches 73
'Here Comes the Bride' 73
Giving away the bride 74
Porch weddings 75
Posh weddings 76
Wedding rings 77
Wedding bracelets 79
Earnest money 79
Luckenbooth 79
The kiss 80
The bridal bouquet 80
The bridal veil 81
The bride stands on the left 83
Lawfully joined together ..84
Father of the bride 85
Mother of the bride 86
The wedding cake 87
Bridal ale 89
The wedding candle 89
Garter tossing 89
Bridesmaids 90
Pageboys and ushers 91
Penny weddings or 'bridewain' 92
Biddings 93
Besom weddings 93
Why almonds? 94
Guard of honour 95
Ribbons on the limo 95

Chapter 5

SUPERSTITIONS

Chimney sweeps 98
'The Chimney Sweeper', from *Songs of Innocence* by William Blake 100
The marriage knot 101
True lovers' knots (*Nodus Herculanus*) 102
Eros/Cupid 102
Tying the knot and getting hitched 103
Handfasting 103
Good and bad omens 105
Horseshoes 107
Tying shoes to the getaway car 108
Slippers and the 'upper hand' 109
Mongolian chicken livers 109
Flowers for weddings 110
Flowers associated with wedding anniversaries .. 112
Names of wedding anniversaries 112
The sex factor 113

Chapter 6

TRADITIONS

Confetti 120
Leap year 121
Bundling 123
Sadie Hawkins Day 125
Gretna Green 126
Queenly proposals 128
Carrying the bride over the threshold 129
Hen nights 130
Brides of Christ 131
Marriage in the early Christian era 132
Droit de seigneur 135
The blood-red wedding .. 135

Chapter 7

HOW IT ALL BEGAN

The concept of marriage . 138
Who came up with the idea? 139
Married women's property rights 141
Marriages in ancient Rome 143
A Roman wedding ... 146
Roman marriage laws . 148
Bride abduction (bride kidnapping) 149
Lord Hardwicke 149
Same-sex marriages 150
Concubinage 155
Polygamy 156
Mormons 156
The Fundamentalist Church of Jesus Christ of Latter-Day Saints 158
Chinese polygamy 159
Polyandry 159
Polygeny 159

Jewish and Islamic rituals 159
Fertility – Jack in the Green 160
Fertility symbols 161

Chapter 8

Afterplay

The first dance 166
Wedding breakfasts 167
Honeymoons 167
Bed 168
Grounds for annulment . .169
Divorce: till debt do us part 170
A vinculo matrimonii 172
Bill of divorcement 172
Wedding anniversaries . . . 173
Threshold 175
Renewal of marriage vows 176
Forced marriages 177
Caxton Hall 178
Widow's weeds 178
Midwives 179
Stay-at-home-husbands . . 180
World wedding statistics . . 180
Longest-lasting marriages 181
Mass weddings 182

Chapter 9

For better, for worse

Afghanistan 186
Amish weddings 186
Australia 187
Bermuda 187
China (Sichuan province) 188
Congo 189
Czechs endorsed 189
Fiji 189
France 190
India 191
The Inuit (Eskimos) 191
Ireland 192
Italy 192
Kenya 193
Korea 193
Marquesas Islands 194
Mauritania 194
Mexico 194
Morocco 194
Native Americans 195
The Navajo 195
The Cherokee 195
The Sioux 196
Poland 197
Puerto Rico 198
Shamanic weddings 198
Spain 199
Sweden 200
Tonga weddings 200
Welsh rare bits 200
Newspaper announcements 201
Prison marriages 202
Conjugal visits 203
Marrying houses 203
Women seeking murderers 204

Bringing home the bacon (The Dunmow Flitch Trials) 205
Marriage anomalies 206
First-night nerves (and other setbacks) 207

Chapter 10
SAME ENDS – DIFFERENT MEANS
Jumping the broom 212
Mehndi parties 212
Paying the ransom *(vykup nevesty)* 213
Showing the face 213
Arranged marriages 214
Hieros gamos: sacred marriage 215
Australian Aborigines 216
Peruvian tradition 217
Papua New Guinea – tribal weddings 217
Pygmy marriages 218
Traditional Chinese weddings 219
Contemporary Chinese weddings 223
Chinese tea ceremony .. 224
Spartan marriages 224
Islamic marriages 226
Gypsy & Romany weddings 227
Hindu marriages 228
Jain marriages 229
Jewish weddings 231
Lebanese weddings 234
Malaysian weddings 235
Maori marriage 235
Quaker weddings 238
Russian weddings 239
Sikh marriages 239
Zulu weddings 241

Chapter 11
THE LAST WORD IN WEDDINGS
Wedding lines 244
Wedlock in literature 254
Jane Austen's era 257

Epilogue 262

APPENDIX 1
Extract from the Decree of the Council of Trent (1563) 265
APPENDIX 2
THE SOLEMNISATION OF MARRIAGE: Extract from *The Directory for Public Worship* (1645) 267
APPENDIX 3
Extract from the Book of Judges 271

Acknowledgements

I am so grateful to Kate Montague for her beautiful artwork, and my thanks to John Blake and his team for their help and encouragement.

Prologue

In the census of AD 2001 over 50 per cent of the population of England and Wales declared themselves to be married.

Ten years later, the Office for National Statistics claimed that this figure had dropped to a mere 45 per cent of the population.

In the 2011 Census of England and Wales, of the total population of 56.1 million, 20.4 million were married and 11.9 per cent claimed to be cohabiting.

In the United States of America only half of the adult population own up to being married.

As soon as my publisher digested these facts, he advised me to get cracking with this book while there are people around who still indulge in matrimony.

BRUCE MONTAGUE
Hove, 2014

Chapter 1

Thinking about it

THE BOTTOM DRAWER
(or HOPE CHEST)

There was an era in the Western world when nearly every unmarried woman would think about preparing for her marriage as soon as she reached her teens. Over the course of several years she would squirrel away clothing and pretty little knick-knacks that she considered would come in handy for married life.

The 'bottom drawer' still preoccupies the imagination of many young ladies the world over, although it is less fashionable to confess it. In the Antipodes it's called the 'glory box'. The Americans call it either the 'hope chest' or 'cedar chest', and in Africa it is known as a 'dowry box'.

It seems likely that in the near future a bride-to-be will collect all she needs in a few hours by shopping on the Internet, if indeed she can't already.

CHOOSING THE RIGHT MONTH

Superstition and tradition pervade everything to do with marriage. Even the months have influence…

Marry when the year is new,
he'll be loving, kind and true
When February birds do mate,
you may wed or dread your fate
If you wed when March winds blow,
joy and sorrow both you'll know

Marry in April when you can,
  joy for maiden and for man
Marry in the month of May,
  you will surely rue the day
Marry when June roses blow,
  over land and sea you'll go
They who in July do wed,
  must labour always for their bread
Whoever wed in August be,
  many a change are sure to see
Marry in September's shine,
  your living will be rich and fine
If in October you do marry,
  love will come, but riches tarry
If you wed in bleak November,
  only joy will come, remember
When December snows fall fast,
  marry and true love will last.

There are alternative rhymes, equally traditional, that advise differently.

Married in January's hoar and rime,
  Widowed you'll be before your prime.
Married in February's sleepy weather,
  Life you'll tread in tune together.
Married when March winds shrill and roar,
  Your home will lie on a distant shore.
Married 'neath April's changeful skies,
  A chequered path before you lies.
Married when bees o'er May blossom flit,
  Strangers around your board will sit.

Married in month of roses – June –
  Life will be one long honeymoon.
Married in July, with flowers ablaze,
  Bitter-sweet mem'ries in after days.
Married in August's heat and drowse,
  Lover and friend in your chosen spouse.
Married in September's golden glow,
  Smooth and serene your life will go.
Married when leaves October thin,
  Toil and hardships for you begin.
Married in veils of November mist,
  Fortune your wedding-ring has kissed.
Married in days of December cheer,
  Love's star shines brighter from year to year.

It would appear that predicting the lucky month depends on finding a decent rhyme. On a more personal basis, this chronicler can put in a kind word for December.

Here's another old saw:

Who marries twixt sickle and scythe
Will never survive.

The doom-laden charmer behind this pathetic couplet had worked out that the sickle was used for the corn harvest and the scythe for the hay harvest. In Europe, the corn harvest is around October and the hay harvest is around July. The question boils down to this: is it best for young couples to avoid the eight months from November to June, or just the two months, August and September? Perhaps he was trying to coincide with the religious sanctions of the time…

DIVINATIONS AND SUPERSTITIONS

May is considered unlucky because it was during this month that the Romans celebrated the Festival of the Dead, the Lemuria (9, 11 and 13 May). Clearly, this makes a marriage in May less than compelling.

It is a popular notion that Juno, the goddess of love and marriage, was honoured by the Romans in June. In fact, one personification of Juno – Juno Moneta – has her festival on 1 June (and another on 10 October), whereas Juno Lucina is celebrated in March. There are other facets of Juno celebrated in February, July and September. It is true, however, that the month of June is named after her.

For religious reasons, certain periods of the year are forbidden for marriage. 'Marry in May and you'll rue the day' was probably coined because the Church disapproved of marriages between Rogation and Whit Sunday. If the forbidden period of Lent is included, and the Church's refusal to marry people between Advent and St Hilary's (13 January), then that leaves only 32 weeks in which to marry. Things used to be more restrictive (see Appendix 2).

St Mark's Eve (26 April) has several superstitions attached. Here's one of them:

> To find out if you or one of your relatives stand a chance of getting married in the coming year, this is what you have to do. Go to a churchyard between 11.00 pm and midnight, and sit on twelve gravestones for five minutes at a time, the final sitting being on a slab opposite the church door. On the FIRST stroke of twelve o'clock, you will see a man enter the church. Stand and watch. On the LAST stroke of midnight, if you see the man come out of the church, then one of your family will soon be

married. However, if the man does not reappear, one of your family will be dead before the next St Mark's Eve.

From *Bye-Gones: Collected from old volumes of folklore* by Richard Holland, 1992

An old practice that seems to have died out (but might be fun to reinstate) was to hang a bell from the springs beneath the bridal bed. If a young lady had no beau on St Valentine's Day, she could pin bay leaves to each corner of her pillow before turning in. Then, in her dreams, her future husband would appear.

ST VALENTINE'S DAY

Each year, on 14 February, men and women send cards and presents to each other declaring their love and, for the most part, they do so anonymously. These days, however, the world is full of young romantics, texting and tweeting their most intimate thoughts.

In ancient Rome, there was a pagan feast to fertility on what would have been 15 February, and the modern practice has evolved from that.

It is as difficult to justify why St Valentine was chosen to be the patron saint of lovers as it is to explain why King Edward III chose St George to be the patron saint of England. St George was a Turkish soldier in the Roman army who showed sympathy to Christians, as a consequence of which he was martyred by the Romans. That was about a thousand years before he became an inspiration to Edward III.

Thirty years prior to St George getting the chop, the Roman Emperor Claudius II held the reins briefly (Claudius Gothicus, AD 268–70). Valentinus (St Valentine, as we call him) had already been lending a sympathetic ear to Christians, which was strictly against Roman law. Indeed, Christian persecution was the order of the day. Valentine, however, was particularly helpful to couples that wished to be blessed in a monotheist, Christian marriage.

The story goes that Valentine was captured and sent to Rome to undergo scrutiny by Claudius II himself. Before long, Claudius took a liking to the renegade. It seems that a grasp of psychology was one of Valentine's weaker points because he was soon tossing aside the Emperor's offer of an olive branch and instead made an attempt to convert Claudius himself to Christianity. This was anathema to Claudius, who immediately ordered Valentine's execution.

Valentine was beaten with clubs, which didn't quite work and so he was stoned. When this did not produce the required effect either, he was escorted, broken but unbowed, without further ado, to the Flaminian Gate on the north road out of Rome, where he was beheaded. This did the trick. Indeed, he was more or less forgotten for the next thousand years.

In 1382, Geoffrey Chaucer wrote a 700-line poem called *Parlement of Foules*, in which he resurrected St Valentine – probably for no better reason than to supersede the pagan holiday of Lupercalia (15 February). His reasoning may have been that if people persisted in celebrating at this particular season of the year, they might as well aspire to some Christian sentiment.

Roughly translated, Valentinus means 'man of valour'. No English church is known to have been dedicated to St Valentine. In America, there is a parish in Cicero, Chicago called St Valentine, founded in 1911. Over the years many hobbies, aspirations and illnesses have been thrust upon the half-forgotten St Valentine for his patronage. Among a dozen other things, he is now the patron saint of lovers, beekeepers, travellers and epileptics.

Regarding the choice of 14 February, in Roman times, the New Year started on the first of March (which is why we are stuck with September, meaning seventh, and October, meaning eighth, and so on). Therefore, February (a corruption of the Latin word *februa*, meaning 'religious purification'), being the last month of the year, was a time for preparing the New Year resolutions. A number of pagan festivals were celebrated to cleanse out the old year: Lupercalia (13–15 February) was a festival dedicated to Juno Februtis, a purifier and fertility goddess. Related to her, according to Ovid, was the goddess of childbirth, Juno Lucina – and connected to both of these were the carnal desires of lusty young men who would write down the names of their objects of desire and submit their prayers to the goddesses; a bit like Valentine cards, really.

The twenty-third of February was considered to be the last day of the old year. And then other days were added to catch up with the lunar year. This was the early equivalent of what we now call 'leap year' (later regularised with the uptake of the Gregorian calendar). The significance of 'leap year' in the lovers' canon is discussed on page 121. There is another common theory as to why 14 February is the day for lovers to plight their troth: it's supposed to be the day when birds begin mating.

In the 17th century, ladies would write down their names on separate pieces of paper, screw them into little balls and leave them in a hat. The men of their acquaintance would pick out a name, and become that lady's valentine for the day. Samuel Pepys records that he had a lot of fun with this lucky lottery. In the year after the Great Fire of London, he found himself the 'valentine' of two ladies. Unfortunately, one of them was his wife. And so to bed.

BRIDAL SHOWERS

Not so long ago, if the father of the bride did not approve of the wedding match, he refused to cough up a dowry for his daughter. Whether this was posturing or penny-pinching, the result was often the same: the bride's family and friends would rally round and 'shower' her with gifts so she could provide her own dowry of sorts and follow through with her intended marriage. In the Western world, formal dowries are rare these days, but the practice of giving 'bridal showers' continues, particularly in America.

THE DOLLY BAG OR WEDDING PURSE (DOROTHY BAG)

The reason why the dolly bag was called a 'Dorothy bag' in the first place lies in the roots of the name. *Doron* in classical Greek can be translated as 'gift', *theos* means 'god'. So the name Dorothea stands for 'gift from God'. Perversely, it was sometimes called 'a Theodora', which is Dorothea rearranged back-to-front but meaning precisely the same thing.

As is noted elsewhere in these pages, symbols of fertility, such as rice and grains, sugar almonds (see Why almonds? page 94) and cake used to be thrown over the couple to wish them luck with speedy propagation. Today, the bride is more likely to use the dolly bag as a fashionable purse in which she can keep items of a personal nature.

THE BANNS

By canon law – that is, ecclesiastical law – the banns have to be announced in church for three consecutive Sundays in advance of the proposed wedding. The point of this is to give ample opportunity for people to object. For example, if someone happens to know that the prospective bride or groom is already married, the three-week banns' period gives the informant a chance to save a poor soul from committing bigamy.

At some point during the wedding ceremony, the priest, or whoever is conducting the proceedings, will generally say, 'If anyone knows cause or just impediment why these two persons should not be joined together in holy matrimony, declare it now or for ever hold your peace.'

Interventions are rare but not unknown. Desperate suitors have resorted to desperate means to woo back their beloved at the eleventh hour. Heavily pregnant women have stepped forward out of the shadows, pointing an accusing finger at the groom. Such interruptions are bound to ruffle the feathers of the participants and take all the fun out of the shindig that follows.

In some parts of Europe, once the third reading of the banns has been completed, the bell-ringers will give a special peal of celebration to announce that the 'big day' is now definitely pencilled into the diary. It's an old tradition called 'the spurring bell'.

Once the banns have been read, the wedding has to be held within three months. Otherwise the engaged couple will have to go through the whole rigmarole again.

RED TAPE BEFORE MARRIAGE

If a couple wish to marry by civil ceremony in a register office or other building approved for civil marriage, they should first contact the superintendent registrar of the district where they wish to marry and discuss the necessary arrangements.

Marriages by Registrar General's Licence are available for when one partner cannot attend a place where marriages can be legally solemnised.

If a couple wishes to be married in church, they should have a discussion with a minister. The Church of England gives everyone with no former partner still living the right to get married in the parish church.

Marriage by Special Licence is rare, and it can only be approved by an Archbishop, and ultimately has to have the authority of the Archbishop of Canterbury.

Marriage by Superintendent Registrar's Certificate without a licence is another method of getting married in accordance with the rites of the Church of England. The applicants must be prepared to be carefully vetted before this is sanctioned.

When a couple consults a superintendent registrar or a church minister to make formal marriage arrangements, each one has to produce proof of identity such as a passport or a birth certificate. Should it be discovered that one of the pair has been married previously, a certificate of decree absolute must be produced. A widow or a widower will have to show the death certificate of the former spouse.

There are statutory fees for getting married in the Church of England or the Church in Wales; which in 2014 amount to a little over £400, which covers the publication of the banns, the certificate of banns and the marriage service (including heating, lighting and administration); additionally, the marriage certificate costs £4.00 at time of registration, and £10.00 subsequently. Other expenses, such as a church choir, bell-ringers, or flowers for the church (if not supplied by a florist), are negotiable. But there is no harm in keeping a smile on the face of the minister in charge.

MARRIAGE BARS

Until the events leading up to the Second World War, it was a widely established practice for women to quit their regular employment, especially teaching and clerical work, on the eve of their marriage. In many cases, a woman would find herself actively banned from working outside the home due to the widely held view that she would have her hands full with her new job as a housewife. This ban on working was officially called 'a marriage bar'. Casual labourers, such as cleaners or child-minders, were less restricted. Certain professions continued to dismiss women upon their marriage until the 1960s. The practice is now unlawful under sex-discrimination legislation.

CLOSED SEASONS FOR CHURCH WEDDINGS

In days of old, there used to be certain times when the church would not allow feasts (weddings) to take place. Some ministers still cling to the old traditions but, in general, they have lapsed.

The prohibited seasons were: from Advent to St Hilary's Day (13 January); Septuagesima to Low Sunday; Rogation Sunday to Trinity Sunday.

For the layman here is a translation: Advent embraces four Sundays beginning with the Sunday nearest to the feast of St Andrew the Apostle (30 November). Septuagesima is the third Sunday before the start of Lent. Low Sunday is the Sunday after Easter. Rogation Sunday is the fifth Sunday after Easter. Trinity Sunday falls one week after Pentecost Sunday, which is also called Whit Sunday and falls 50 days after Easter.

The early Church was sometimes willing to ignore the 'closed seasons' by charging more for permitting marriages to take place during these periods.

The Roman Catholic Church continues an embargo on marriages between the first Sunday of Advent and the Octave of the Epiphany (the eight days from 6 to 13 January), and from Ash Wednesday (46 days before Easter) to Low Sunday.

In the Protestant church there are no canonical restrictions today.

THE ART OF COURTLY LOVE

From *The Art of Courtly Love* by Andreas Capellanus (*c.* 1185):

Thou shalt avoid avarice like the deadly pestilence and shalt embrace its opposite.
Thou shalt keep thyself chaste for the sake of her whom thou lovest.
Thou shalt not knowingly strive to break up a correct love affair that someone else is engaged in.
Thou shalt not chose for thy love anyone whom a natural sense of shame forbids thee to marry.
Be mindful completely to avoid falsehood.
Thou shalt not have many who know of thy love affair.
Being obedient in all things to the commands of ladies, thou shalt ever strive to ally thyself to the service of Love.
In giving and receiving love's solaces let modesty be ever present.
Thou shalt speak no evil.
Thou shalt not be a revealer of love affairs.
Thou shalt be in all things polite and courteous.
In practising the solaces of love thou shalt not exceed the desires of thy lover.

The above was written in Latin by Andreas Capellanus at, it

is believed, his mistress's request, for the edification of a man called Walter. We don't know much about Walter but if he took the advice to heart he was a wise and lucky fellow. Capellanus was serving at the time as chaplain for the Court of Marie, Countess of Champagne, daughter of Eleanor of Aquitaine. The piece was widely quoted and became the template for many as to how a gentleman in love should conduct himself.

Many elements of courtly love exist to this day but, alas, not many of the sentiments are adhered to.

The concept of courtly love is perhaps exemplified in the love affair between Lancelot and Guinevere (although, worryingly, she was married to King Arthur at the time).

FREE LOVE AND LOVE BEADS

In the counterculture of the 1960s and 1970s, the 'free-love movement' became associated in the public mind with promiscuity. 'Sex radical' was the term preferred by proponents at the time because of the negative connotations of 'free love'. By whatever name, advocates had two strong beliefs: 1) the opposition to any idea of coerced sexual activity in a relationship; and 2) the right of women to use their bodies in whatever way they please.

There was a serious purpose behind the movement. Marriage was seen as a form of social bondage but sex radicals were not advocating multiple sexual partners. The rationale was that matters of love and commitment were personal and should not be manipulated by the state. Love beads became symbolic of the movement. Easily made and redolent of more primitive cultures and purer beliefs, love beads, usually in two strings, were worn by both men and women on a necklace, especially by hippies, as a symbol of love and peace.

Chapter 2

Leading up to it

CHOOSING THE RIGHT DAY

As with choosing the right month in the previous chapter, the response to 'which day?' is steeped in hoary superstition. As the saying goes, marry on a:

Monday – brides will be healthy
Tuesday – brides will be wealthy
Wednesday – brides do best of all
Thursday – brides will suffer losses
Friday – brides will suffer crosses
Saturday – brides will have no luck at all.

Friday the 13th is unlucky for a number of reasons: first, it's said that the 13th person to turn up at the Last Supper, Judas, upset the apple cart. Second, it takes 13 treads to ascend the steps of the hangman's scaffold. Thirdly, a coven of witches consists of 13 women. Fourth, in a deck of Tarot cards, Number 13 depicts the Grim Reaper – that is, Death. Fifthly, the blade of the guillotine used in France during the Reign of Terror (1793–94) had a drop of 13 feet. And coincidentally, it is alleged that the car in which Princess Diana was killed collided with the 13th pillar of the tunnel at Place de l'Alma, Paris.

In the 16th century, the most suitable day for a wedding was considered to be a Sunday. There were also different times of the year to be considered:

If you marry in Lent
You will live to repent
Marry in May
Rue for aye

(in this case, 'aye' is a Scottish
word meaning 'ever')

Until the mid-Victorian era, Christmas Day was one of the few holidays enjoyed by the working classes and so it became a popular day on which to get married, but the leisured classes turned very sanctimonious about it.

Until the Liberal MP John Lubbock introduced a bill in 1871 there were only two national holidays observed in England, Wales and Ireland: Christmas Day and Good Friday. Lubbock introduced four more holidays: Easter Monday, Whit Monday, Boxing Day and the first Monday in August, thereby increasing the days on which working people could be married.

Hogmanay (according to some, derived from the Old French word *aguillanneuf* – meaning last day of the year) seemed a lively way of getting a marriage celebration up and running. The canny Scots spotted the magic ingredient early on and developed a penchant for marrying on New Year's Day.

In the 21st century, Saturday is the most popular day to have a wedding, with Friday coming a close second.

He's a fule that marries at Yule
For when the bairn's to bear
The corn's to shear.

(Denham Tracts 1895)

That ancient poet just wouldn't give up trying.

THE ENGAGEMENT

To get engaged is a mere formality – it's not essential. Many a wedding has taken place because of a spur-of-the-moment decision, particularly in Las Vegas. The benefits of an engagement include not only giving the couple a breathing space to ensure the seriousness of their commitment but also enough time to plan properly for the Big Day. Often it is necessary to book six months in advance to secure the right venue and a suitable caterer.

The longest engagement on record was between Octavio Guillen and Adriana Martinez in Mexico. After 'dating' for 67 years, they finally got married. We are not told whether the bride had 'saved herself' for the occasion.

ENGAGEMENT RINGS

Ancient Egyptians presented their intended brides with circlets of rushes and hemp. It has been suggested that these symbolised the remnants of ropes that bound the wrists of the captured women of a previous, more savage age. The husband would wrap his wife's ankles and wrists with ropes of hay in the belief this would keep her spirit within her. Once she had been tamed and submitted more willingly to him, the theory is he tied a piece of string around her finger to remind her of the bonds she once wore. It was only in later times that two rings materialised, one for the engagement and one for the marriage, the engagement ring given as the groom's pledge.

The engagement ring as we think of it now was first introduced during the Anglo-Saxon period. It was fashioned from crude metal and symbolised eternal love. Later, rich folk set a small diamond into it, ostensibly for its hardness and durability, but more likely because of its lasting value. Indeed, such rings have become heirlooms.

The modern custom of setting a diamond in the ring was introduced within the past 100 years. This was the consequence of a sustained advertising campaign by the diamond company, De Beers, in the 1930s, when it was said that the cost of one of their rings was the equivalent of two months' salary for a man on an average wage.

If a swain intends to bend the knee and hand over an engagement ring on the spot, it would be wise for him to hang onto the receipt: not on the off chance that his proposal will be given the bum's rush but because his beloved's taste in jewellery might differ from his. The engagement ring is usually a diamond solitaire, which is symbolic of love and eternity. Some ladies prefer an alternative stone – a ruby or an emerald, perhaps. Ordinarily, the gem is set in gold although platinum is harder wearing and is, if anything, more avant-garde.

If the suitor makes his proposition by slipping the ring onto her left hand while crumpling the receipt into the other, she can say 'yes' gracefully before dashing off to exchange his gift for a ring of her choice. It's all part of the lessons a man has to learn in order to know what it really feels like to be 'the mister' in the mister and missus package.

Until the 19th century, a fiancée wore the engagement ring on her right hand and only transferred it to her left hand upon marriage.

PRINCESS DIANA'S ENGAGEMENT RING

On 24 February 1981, Princess Diana's engagement to Prince Charles got off to a flying start when she chose a £30,000 ring consisting of 14 solitaire diamonds surrounding a 12-carat oval blue Ceylon sapphire, set in 18-carat white gold.

Despite this, when she was making her vows during the service, she muddled up her husband's name, saying, 'Philip Charles Arthur George' instead of 'Charles Philip Arthur George'.

In October 2010, whilst on holiday in Kenya, Prince William (now the Duke of Cambridge), gave Catherine 'Kate' Middleton this same sapphire ring that his father, Prince Charles, had given his mother.

PRECIOUS STONES – THEIR SYMBOLISM

The taste in jewellery changes over the years. Originally, in medieval times, attributions were given to everything, including precious stones. For what it's worth, here is a list compiled in the Victorian era, but the meanings stem from the Middle Ages. Anyone wearing a stone or a combination of them was trying to say something about himself or herself, mirroring a particular virtue:

Chrysoprase:	*Virtue*
Red Jasper:	*Love*
Beryl:	*Purification*
Green Jasper:	*Faith*
White Jasper:	*Gentleness*
Amethyst:	*Christ's martyrdom*
Chalcedony:	*Closeness to God*
Emerald:	*Christian hope*
Sardonyx:	*Chastity or humility*
Chrysolite:	*Heavenly life*
Sapphire:	*Heaven-bound*
Hyacinth:	*God's grace*

KNEELING TO PROPOSE

The uncomfortable custom of a suitor getting down on bended knee to make a proposal of marriage hearkens back to jousting tournaments. A knight would kneel before his chosen lady and beg her to allow him to compete as her champion under her standard or colours, which he would wear on his epaulette or helmet. With the horseman on one knee it was easier for the lady to place her scarf or token on his shoulder.

Out of incidental interest, actors are wished good luck by being told to 'break a leg'. This means bowing or 'bending the knee'. In other words, the well-wisher is hoping the actor will receive applause, in response to which the performer will gladly 'break a leg' or 'bend the knee.'

SEX MANUALS FOR THE YOUNG BRIDE

Men and women have always wanted to learn about sex. Part of the fun of getting married is to put the theory into practice. An anonymous publication appeared in 1684 called *Aristotle's Compleat Master-Piece*. One of the first practical books on the subject, it has nothing to do with the Greek philosopher who allegedly taught Alexander the Great a thing or two.

Composed anonymously, its chief claim to fame is the proposition that during sexual intercourse, the greater the intensity of the female orgasm the greater will be the probability of pregnancy. There are a great many more titbits in the book that can help to satisfy a married couple's desire to get to the nub of the matter. Though it was banned in 1768, it never lost its popularity under the covers. It is now available through Amazon so that couples can Kindle it in bed.

A century ago, books were coy in their approach to informing young women about their maturing bodies. In

1919, one of the most daring was called *What the Flower Teaches Us*. A primary concern of early sex educators was to warn young people of the evils of masturbation. This fear, happily, appears to have been shaken off.

Such manuals as *The Lesbian Sex Book* by Wendy Caster (Alyson Publications, 1993) have brought things to a head. Other books include, *She Comes First: The Thinking Man's Guide to Pleasuring the Woman*, by Ian Kerner (Souvenir Press, 2005), and *Passionate Marriage: Keeping Love and Intimacy Alive in Committed Relationships*, by David Schnarch (W.W. Norton & Company).

These days, the World Wide Web is the bride and groom's oyster. Even so, what is left to the imagination is limitless, which lends mystery to a successful marriage. For those dedicated to this sort of research, getting down on one knee and proposing is the surest way towards fulfilment.

There is a book soon to be published called *Birds, Bees and Educated Fleas*. They all do it, and this book will explain how they do it. There will also be a chapter on the human endeavour. Worth putting aside for a dolly bag, I think.

CHURCH OR CIVIL?

By law, a marriage must take place between 8am and 6pm except for Quaker weddings or those in the Jewish faith, which require special licences.

Humanist ceremonies have no legal standing and require a re-affirmation of vows in a register office to become valid. Otherwise, the solemnisation needs to be verified by an ordained minister of a recognised religion, or a superintendent registrar. Scientologists also have problems finding a lawful venue.

If one partner is Jewish and the other isn't, then the rabbi cannot perform a marriage service unless the non-Jewish person converts to Judaism.

THE BRIDE'S LIST

Once the bride has said 'yes', the race is on. Her responsibilities include preparing the 'theme' of the wedding, the invitations, the cake, the flowers, the organisation of the bridesmaids and any others whom she wishes to join her on the Big Day. Traditionally, Mum and Dad pay for the bride's dress and the outfits worn by the bridesmaids and pageboys. They also pay the lion's share of the contribution towards the cost of the reception, the drinks and the transport.

Increasingly in the UK, however, couples are paying for their own weddings. In 2013, it was estimated that the average cost of a wedding in the UK was £20,000. The report (by VoucherCodesPro) suggested that couples are delaying the day of marriage by three years in order to save up for it.

THE GROOM'S LIST

The prospective husband usually forks out rather more than the bride. He has to obtain the licence, pay the many necessary fees and ensure all the paperwork is filled in correctly. He has to choose his best man, buy the wedding ring, and stand guarantee for the best man's bills including limos, ushers and the stag night. He is also responsible for the banns being called, and for ordering the choir and the bell-ringers and paying for their services.

CHANGING THE SURNAME

A married woman can legally take her husband's name as her own, but she is not legally compelled to do so. Some women prefer to retain an aura of independence and, once the ceremony is over, continue to use their maiden name. A compromise is to use both names and link them with a hyphen. When a woman does adopt her husband's name, she must inform the authorities, which include those dealing with her insurance, passport, driving licence, et cetera.

COMMON-LAW MARRIAGE

Common-law marriage has also had the legal title of 'marriage by cohabitation with habit and repute'. (Common law is the part of English law that 'derives from custom and judicial precedent, rather than statutes', and is found in some other countries, including the USA, Australia, Canada, India and Ireland),

It is commonly believed that if a couple live together for seven years, they have proved their bond to such an extent that their union is, de facto, a common-law marriage. This is a fallacy.

In law, there is a long-held presumption that even though there was no appointed official or recognised minister officiating, if a couple *believe* they are married then, in some jurisdictions, those two people are recognized as being married.

Some countries and certain American states recognise common-law marriage. For common-law marriages to be waved through (they're tolerated only grudgingly), the couple a) would have had to be legally free to marry, b) would have had to prove they had proper consent, c) physically cohabit, d) lead a domiciled life as a couple, and e) encourage the community in which they live to assume they are married.

In other words, if two people call themselves a married

couple they may get away with it amongst their neighbours, but when it comes to filing tax returns and claiming child benefit, it would simplify everybody's lives if they just went through a quick civil marriage ceremony in front of a Justice of the Peace with a couple of witnesses.

MARRIAGE BY SHIPS' CAPTAINS

One of the few countries to condone marriage at sea is Bermuda, although the officiator, who might be the captain of the vessel, needs to obtain a temporary licence in advance. Couples wishing to marry must be over 21. They also have to give notice of their intention before sailing, and provide birth certificates and other documentation.

No major country in the world has a provision in law for marriage on board a ship in international waters other than through the offices of a valid religious minister or a qualified state official. On rare occasions, the captain may be qualified by virtue of being, in his own right, a minister or a rabbi or a JP or a public notary. But if he holds such qualifications, why on earth is he captaining a boat?

Japanese ships allow their captains to perform marriage ceremonies at sea but only if the couple involved are bona fide Japanese citizens. Even then, the newly-weds will have to reaffirm their vows once back on terra firma.

The Code of Federal Regulations in the USA (known as 32 CFR 700.716) prints the following ruling:

> The commanding officer shall not perform a marriage ceremony on board his ship or aircraft. He shall not permit a marriage ceremony to be performed on board when the ship or aircraft is outside the territory of the United States, except: (a) In accordance with local laws

… and (b) In the presence of a diplomatic or consular official of the United States.

For all that, the idea persists that a couple can go on a cruise and, somewhere far out at sea, on the spur of the moment, ask the captain to marry them. Some cruise ships carry a notice showing words to the following effect: 'Any marriages performed by the captain of this ship are valid for the duration of this trip only.'

There have been exceptional circumstances where marriages have been performed without the presence of a recognised official. These are called 'emergency weddings' – carried out where the lives of one or both of the pro-posed spouses are endangered. If one should die before a JP or a minister can be contacted, then legal sanctioning must be obtained at a later date to validate the marriage… Not that this is of much use to the deceased, of course, whose marriage could probably be nullified due to non-consummation.

LAS VEGAS WEDDINGS

Many celebrities have been married in Las Vegas: Elvis Presley, Frank Sinatra, Bruce Willis, Michael Jordan, Britney Spears, et cetera. A-list, B-list and Z-list stars have married there. In fact, more than 120,000 weddings every year are conducted in Las Vegas. It is the favourite venue for tying the knot in the US.

It is estimated that a white wedding in America will cost a minimum of $20,000 (£12,000). However, in Las Vegas you can get hitched on the spur of the moment for less than $1,000 (£600). Just make sure you collect a couple of witnesses as you walk into a licensed wedding venue.

Some might perceive it as a disadvantage that some of the wedding chapels in Las Vegas have a conveyor-belt mentality, particularly in the hotels. Whilst biding their time before going into the little chapel, brides and grooms may well find themselves in the company of several other couples waiting in the queue. After the ceremony, they might have to run the gauntlet between the gaming tables, gamely trying to resist temptation at craps, roulette or blackjack.

A SHORT LIST OF CONFUSING DEFINITIONS

Betrothal and Espousal

Betrothed and betrothal are ancient words meaning 'an engagement to get married', from Medieval English: 'be troth'. Troth is the old form of True Oath meaning in effect, swearing to be truthful; to honour a promise. Espousal comes from the Old French word meaning 'the act of betrothal' (see Espousal, further down).

Bridezilla

Refers to a woman who arranges her own wedding with single-minded enthusiasm and whereby outsiders consider her behaviour obsessive or extreme. The male equivalent is called a groomzilla, and is quite common in street slang.

Civil Marriage

This refers to a marriage officiated by someone from the State as opposed to someone from the Church. Those getting hitched in a civil ceremony may have to contend with baffling logic. Here is a case in point.

In the UK, since 1837, hymns and Bible readings have

been banned from civil marriage ceremonies. In February 2013, barrister Mr Gary Lidington, together with his fiancée Louise, began preparations for a civil ceremony to be held at the end of June at Wilton's Music Hall in Whitechapel. The ensuing four months were spent arranging the ceremony in meticulous detail. On the night before the wedding, the couple received a message from the registrar of Tower Hamlets (whose auspices include Whitechapel) to say that the phrase 'in sickness and in health' could not be legally used as it was 'too religious'. Instead, the words 'in sickness and when we are well' had to be substituted. In addition, the couple were forbidden to use the words, 'to have and to hold'. However, the Council deemed it acceptable for them to say, 'to hold and to have'.

Tower Hamlets later issued this statement: 'We apologise for the short notice Mr and Mrs Lidington received regarding changes to their chosen vows. It was important their civil ceremony complied with the legal process.'

Yet another case to add as back-up to Charles Dickens's wry observation in *Oliver Twist* that 'the Law is a ass – a idiot'.

Commitment Ceremony

Particularly used in same-sex unions. This is a ceremony similar to a civil union between two people of the same sex who do not choose to marry, but it has no legal status, and does not have to be performed by a registrar.

Domestic Partnership

Some people simply don't believe in a formal marriage. They desire to live together without making promises to anybody or about anything. Some jurisdictions, such as Australia, New Zealand and the American states of California, Nevada,

Oregon and Washington accept couples that set themselves up as 'a domestic partnership' in much the same way as they would if they were formally married.

In common law spouses in common-law marriages (see above) may protect themselves by means of a legal instrument, imposed by a court in the event of a dispute over property resulting from a partnership, known as a Constructive Trust. One purpose of forming a domestic partnership is to safeguard each partner's contribution to the property of the other. Some jurisdictions have instituted domestic partnerships as a means of recognising same-sex unions.

ESPOUSAL

Until the Council of Trent (1563 – see Appendix 1), in Ireland particularly, the usual mode of contracting marriages was by espousal (theologically referred to as '*sponsalia de futuro*') in which the couple said, 'I *will* take thee to be…' et cetera. The espousal was accompanied by the sacerdotal benediction and when the time specified by the parties had elapsed, the marriage became contractually binding without resorting to a contract *'de praesenti'*, in which the couple said, 'I *do* take thee…' et cetera.

The difference is semantic. In the first case, the wording is dependent on being in the future tense, creating a promise (I will). In the second case, 'I do' being in the present tense, creates a verbal contract – a commitment.

The espousal could be declared null and void if either couple were found guilty of heresy, renunciation of their faith, infidelity or disfigurement.

MAIL-ORDER BRIDE

A company specialising in brokering marriages is paid in order to bring a woman from another country for the purpose of matrimony. Some of these arrangements are so common they have developed the generic name of 'Philippine brides'.

MARRIAGE/MATRIMONY

The word 'marriage' was formed in the 13th century. It derives from the Latin word *matrimonium*, combining '*mater*', meaning mother, with the suffix, 'monium', signifying action or condition.

MARRIAGE BONDS

Marriage bonds are obsolete, but they used to be useful to those who could afford them in order to by-pass the banns (see page 25) and, sometimes, to avoid legitimate objections to a marriage.

A 'special licence' could be obtained from a bishop for various legitimate reasons such as the necessity for speed or privacy. To secure a special licence, the purchaser had to sign a 'marriage bond' promising to indemnify the Bishop should an impediment to the marriage be discovered later, which had not been declared when the licence was issued. The price paid to the Bishop for this licence was about £200, a sum far higher than ordinary folk could afford.

Marriage bonds and allegations (the document in which the couple alleged, or the groom alleged on behalf of both, that there were no impediments to the marriage) only existed for those couples that applied to marry by licence. They did not exist for couples that were married by banns. In fact, the real reason for their existence may have been to lessen discovery of bigamous intent, and the Church was not so naïve as to be unaware of this. After 1823 marriage bonds were no longer available.

Marriage licence

The marriage licence is an official document that two people need to obtain in order to get married.

TO PLIGHT ONE'S TROTH

The phrase means to pledge one's sacred oath to a promise of marriage.

In the traditional marriage ceremony (from the 1662 Church of England 'Book of Common Prayer') the following words are said by the groom:

> I [NAME] take thee [NAME] to be my wedded Wife, to have and to hold from this day forward, for better for worse, for richer for poorer, in sickness and in health, to love, cherish, and to obey, till death us do part, according to God's holy ordinance; and thereto I plight thee my troth.

Shoshbin

A Hebrew word meaning 'a close friend'. In the Aramaic language it is the equivalent of the 'best man' at a gentile wedding.

Spouse

Spouse is merely a gender-neutral term meaning either the male or the female partner in a marriage, a civil union, a domestic partnership or common-law marriage.

Shotgun wedding

The phrase is an American colloquialism. When the father of a pregnant woman decides that the man responsible for getting his daughter into that condition must do the decent thing and marry her, there may be some initial resistance.

It has been known that under such circumstances an angry father might resort to coercion, threatening his putative son-in-law with a shotgun, and forcing him to go through with the marriage ceremony. This cosy scenario has come to be referred to as 'A Shotgun Wedding'. Such threatening behaviour is no longer legal in the US, but there are a number of folk songs that recall many weddings of this nature in recent history. And several others where the recalcitrant groom has ended up on Boot Hill buried amongst gunmen who discovered too late that they were just a smidgen too slow on the draw.

In the 21st century, as the stigma attached to single-motherhood fades, out-of-wedlock births increase exponentially. Access to methods of birth control and the availability of legal abortion give women independence and choice. Some women prefer to give birth and bring up a child unfettered by male influence.

The Universal Declaration of Human Rights states that a woman's right to choose a spouse and enter freely into marriage is central to her dignity and equality as a human being.

Special Licence

There are occasions when two people need to get married at a time or a place that would not normally be covered by the official authorities. This sometimes happens, for example, when a soldier is sent overseas at short notice. At such times, it is possible to secure a 'special licence' to overcome red tape.

Lord Byron was married by special marriage licence because, he claimed, he wanted to avoid a 'fashionable wedding.' A cursory examination of Lord Byron's love life might lead the sceptically minded to wonder if he had other reasons to duck under the radar. Charles Dickens obtained a special licence from the Vicar General's office in Doctors' Commons (a place that will be instantly recollected by readers of *The Pickwick Papers*). Dickens's marriage licence consisted of an address written on vellum from the Archbishop of Canterbury to his 'trusty, well-beloved Charles Huffam Dickens and Catherine Hogarth', enabling them to be married at any time or place without banns. Fame sometimes has its advantages.(Catherine was not quite 21 at the time Dickens wanted to marry her; hence he had to secure a special marriage licence.)

Failing to obtain a special licence could have devastating consequences. William Shakespeare's youngest daughter, Judith, got married to Mr Thomas Quiney on 10 February 1616, which fell into the Lenten season of Shrovetide (28 January–7 April), thus needing a special licence from the Bishop of Worcester. Apparently, the Vicar of Stratford took it upon himself to suggest this was not absolutely necessary, so Quiney didn't bother to present himself at the consistory court to collect the licence. As a consequence, he was excommunicated on 12 March 1616.

William Shakespeare was not best pleased. A day or so after the excommunication, Quiney's name was scratched out as a beneficiary from Shakespeare's will and the words 'daughter Judyth' substituted. Shakespeare was to die after his somewhat raucous 52nd birthday party three weeks later (21 April 1616).

Though William didn't live to see it, the good news was that the ban was lifted in time for the Quineys to baptise the late William Shakespeare's first grandchild (with the Christian name of Shakespeare) on 23 November 1616.

Trousseau

This is a term, from a French word meaning 'bundle', that covers all the accoutrements (clothes, linen, and so on) that the bride will need for the day of her marriage.

THE WEDDING INDUSTRY

Along with a surge in secular marriages, couples have taken to composing their own vows to such an extent that today there are websites devoted solely to writing personalised vows. At the mere touch of a screen, prospective newly-weds can communicate with wedding specialists who deal in everything from bridal shows and venue planning to historically-themed dresses, dressmakers, formalwear hire companies, florists, caterers, cake makers, decorators, confetti distributors, photographers, printers, chimney sweeps and travel firms with exotic locations.

Chapter 3

Foreplay

SOMETHING OLD, SOMETHING NEW

The old adage, describing what a bride should wear for luck at her wedding, is often left incomplete. A part of the original triolet (a poem of eight lines with a fixed rhyme scheme) goes:

> Something old, something new,
> Something borrowed, something blue,
> And a silver sixpence in her shoe.

Something old is generally something passed down from mother to daughter – sometimes going back generations, often a piece of jewellery. It signifies a continuing connection with the bosom of her family.

Something new is, nowadays, most likely to be the wedding dress. It signifies starting anew. Something borrowed is part of the trousseau signifying that the bride to be has faithful friends who will remain close no matter what.

Something blue may be hidden in her underclothing or it may be a garter, but its significance goes back to the Virgin Mary, who is most often portrayed wearing a blue mantle. Blue is the colour of the sky and therefore the gateway to heaven; it is the painter's symbol of purity.

A silver sixpence in her shoe used to be represented by a small coin. This signified that the bride would never be penniless. The sixpence was a small silver English coin first minted in the reign of Edward VI (1551).

Here's an old trick used by some actors. They put a coin in one of their shoes for this reason: the niggle caused by the bump in the shoe is sufficiently distracting to lessen their first-night nerves. Perhaps such methodology also helped a highly strung young bride to sail through the wedding ceremony with equanimity, although it is to be hoped that she retained a vestige of dignity by removing her shoes before her first night.

THE SHOW OF PRESENTS

In Scotland, the bride's mother would hold an 'open house' for the wedding gifts. After they were unwrapped and displayed, the bride was often dressed up and carried aloft through the streets accompanied by much singing and merriment.

In the 16th and 17th centuries, wedding guests who brought presents were rewarded with pairs of gloves. Sometimes hundreds of pairs were given away. An expert on folklore (George Monger) postulates that the symbolism of gloves may be 'to extend the hand of friendship'.

THE WEDDING GUEST BOOK

Once upon a time, all the guests attending a wedding were considered to be witnesses and were obliged to sign the marriage document. The wedding guest book, therefore, was essential to keep track of the witnesses. It has outlived that use now and is instead an item of nostalgia for a couple, where they can look back to the day they took the big step towards togetherness.

THE BEST MAN (OR GROOMSMAN)

Imagine a chargé d'affaires in a hostile middle-Eastern country opposed to democracy. That situation is analogous to the position of a best man at a wedding. His primary concern is damage limitation; his second is diplomacy. The best man is the groom's reliable and trustworthy confidant. In Jewish marriages, he is called the Shoshbin (see page 47).

To find the origins, we have to go back hundreds of years, to the time when merciless Huns, Goths and Vandals swept across Asia Minor and Europe, pillaging and raping en route. Before Christianity gained ground on the Continent, the subjugation of women was very much a fact of life. Even after the moral values of the Catholic Church began to take hold, those primal needs of a man to secure a mate continued with few scruples. Where women were in short supply, the single man, frustrated with bachelorhood, would organise marauding raids on neighbouring communities to capture a potential bride. This strong-arm approach required backup, so the bachelor would bring along a 'best man' who would act as lookout and 'muscle'.

Over the centuries, such brutality has softened into cosy folklore. But in those dark days, there was always the threat of reprisal when the bride's tribe would send out a raiding party to recapture their woman by force. In such a situation, the best man's continued vigilance became a matter of life or death. Armed and alert, he maintained a presence as chief bodyguard throughout the marriage ceremony and during the subsequent 'honeymonth' (see Honeymoons, page 167).

In the old days, the best man was invariably a bachelor. Charles Dickens asked his publisher, John Macrone, to be his best man when he married Catherine Hogarth, but Macrone's American wife intervened and insisted that a best man must be single. They married in Chelsea at St Luke's church where Charles Kingsley's son was rector. Thomas Beard, a fellow journalist with whom Dickens had worked on the *Morning Herald* ended up as the best man.

To sum up, the role of being best man or best friend and bodyguard really hasn't changed. He's still there to protect the groom on his stag night; to ensure the groom isn't compromised by some stripper pretending to be a policewoman; to ensure he gets enough sleep in the eight hours before the marriage ceremony, and, above all, to safeguard the wedding ring. Traditionally the best man is supposed to carry a lucky mascot in his pocket and once the ceremony has commenced he must not, under any circumstances leave to go home.

Finally, at the bun fight afterwards, the best man is supposed to remain sober enough to make a sparkling speech in which he is allowed to introduce inoffensive innuendo.

THE BEST MAN'S CHECKLIST

The best man may find it easier to share the burden of going through this checklist in association with the maid (or matron) of honour (often called chief bridesmaid in the UK). There are 24 essential points to be ticked off. On the day, the best man will find approximately 3,452 more to add.

1) The ring.
2) Put the ushers on stand-by.
3) Collect hire-clothes.
4) Boutonnières.
5) Stag night guest list & surprises.
6) The ring.
7) Order the honeymoon transport

8) Arrange transport to get groom to wedding.
9) Get dressed.
10) Help groom to get dressed.
11) The ring.
12) Escort groom to venue
13) Give ring to the service giver.
14) Get everybody to turn off mobile phones.
15) Sign register as witness.
16) Organise photographs.
17) Gratuities and marriage fees.
18) Ensure the newly-weds get to the reception.
19) As the last speaker, make the end speech hilarious.
20) Act as toastmaster.
21) Sober up.
22) Arrange for wedding presents be put in safe place.
23) Phone getaway limousines for father of bride.
24) Remember to switch on mobile phone.

THE WOODEN SPOON

There is a tradition, now on its last legs, of presenting a wooden spoon, often intricately carved, to the bride. When domestication was more prevalent than it is today, the wooden spoon was valued highly as an essential utensil in the kitchen. The expectations of the average bride were to feed her fledgling family and do her duty with the limited resources that her chosen man could provide.

There were regional variations. In Scotland, for example, a spurtle, used for stirring porridge, was a popular gift to a budding housewife.Other lucky tokens include shoes, bells, wishbones, black cats and rolling pins, normally hung around the body in decorative form.

THE BOUTONNIERE

In the days of chivalry, medieval knights jousted on behalf of a lady by wearing her colours. Today, the groom wears a flower in his buttonhole often made to match one in his bride's bouquet. The bride's father and the ushers also wear buttonholes, but these will differ from the groom's.

THE THISTLE

A Scotsman's boutonnière might not be a flower but a thistle, representing the symbol of good luck and independence.

In the days of King Malcolm I of Scotland (943–54), when Danes were constantly shipping over from Scandinavia and invading the east coast of Britain, Malcolm posted sentries on the coastal moors, where his men slept amongst the gorse bushes. One dark night, the Danes disembarked and crept ashore. The hardy Scottish vigilantes were quickly awakened by the cries of Danes screaming with pain as their naked feet trod on thistles. The Scottish militia, wearing clogs, drove the Danes back into the sea. Ever since, the thistle has been used as the Scottish emblem. The pain of Danes was plainly music to the Thanes.

TUXEDOS

In England, best men and other males acquainted with the groom, including the groom himself, have been known to question why, when getting kitted out for a wedding, they are often expected to go to the expense of hiring dinner jackets, or 'tuxedos', as gentlemen's outfitters call them these days, although traditional wedding attire for men is morning dress, consisting of a tail coat, waistcoat and striped trousers, usually accompanied by a top hat, either black or grey.

Until 1884, most formal evening wear for men consisted

of a long tailcoat, white waistcoat and white tie. The Prince of Wales (known as Bertie to his friends and later as King Edward VII) persuaded his tailor to make him a formal coat without 'a tail' so that he could have a more comfortable 'seat' when saddled up and riding a horse on fox hunts.

An American tobacco magnate called Pierre Lorillard caught sight of this new style of jacket and liked it so much he had something similar tailored in his hometown. He lived 40 miles north of New York City. The land he owned had been acquired from the Algonquin Indian tribe and was called *P'tauk-seet-dough*, meaning 'Home of the Bear'. Spoken phonetically, this Indian place name is pronounced 'tuxedo'.

In October 1886, there was a Grand Ball at the Tuxedo Club in Tuxedo Park, an area of New York State that Pierre Lorillard had developed as his personal sporting estate. It is possible that Lorillard decided that to wear his new tail-less jacket was too radical a departure for conventional society. However, he had a son – Griswold – who, it seems, had something of Jay Gatsby about him. At any rate, Griswold and a few of his cronies sported themselves in these unconventional jackets and, by all accounts, wowed the crowd with their elegance. The word spread, and soon tuxedos became de rigueur at formal occasions.

There is a saying that whatever new fashion takes off in America will take root in England six months later. That is what happened to the tuxedo – and why men's clothes shops now hire out so many of them for weddings in place of morning dress, a fashion that seems to have started on the Continent; in France, for instance, men often wear tuxedos to formal weddings.

THE MARRIAGE CERTIFICATE

The marriage does not become a legally binding contract until both parties sign the marriage certificate in front of witnesses. For convenience this is invariably done in the presence of all parties immediately after the ceremony.

The certificate given to the bride is 'a certified copy of an entry of marriage' in the registers. It is not necessary for it to bear the actual signatures of the couple, the witnesses and the officiating minister so long as their signatures are transcribed.

MARRIAGE REGISTERS

Identical entries should be made in two registers. The registrar's 'Guidance for the Clergy with reference to the Marriage and Registration Acts' states: 'In no circumstances should an entry in a register be commenced until the marriage has been legally completed.'

When the duplicate registers are full, one copy is sent to the Registrar General and the other either kept in the church or sent to the Diocesan Registry of Deeds.

Even today, if the minister or registrar fills in the registers incorrectly, he risks a jail sentence of 14 years.

WEDDING FAVOURS

Called *bomboniere* (sugar sweets) in Italy, wedding favours originated, traditionally, as five sugared almonds, coloured white for a wedding, and given as gifts to wedding guests. One is for health, the second for wealth and the third for long life. The fourth is for happiness and the fifth is for fertility.

They are usually presented in delicately covered satin bags and tied with ribbons to co-ordinate with the colours of the bridesmaids' dresses. The bride often gives them as gifts to her five 'ladies in waiting'.

Favours are also served on such special occasions as baptism and bar mitzvahs. *Bomboniere* (known by the Greeks as *konfeta*) traditionally consist of Jordan almonds, almonds coated in a sugar glaze, often in different colours.

LOVE TOKENS

Courtship has engendered the giving of love tokens throughout history. In days gone by it might have been a beautifully carved needle case or a shuttle. Ornate wedding chests were often given to the bride. A double spoon, symbolising a bountiful union, was traditional in England. In the former Czechoslovakia painted eggs or carved sticks were popular. Bed curtains and bedspreads decorated with symbolic figures from the Garden of Eden, and mating birds are still deemed appropriate. Two halves of a coin, one for him and one for her, were sufficient tokens of love for the very poor.

TO PRE-NUP OR NOT PRE-NUP?

With the prevalence of divorce these days, pre-nuptial agreements are on the increase. If either party has anything to lose, a previously agreed understanding seems the least hurtful course should the shine rub off the romance. At the time of the wedding when the two young people are feverishly in love, they are probably unlikely to feel any need to pay for a legal agreement detailing who gets a slice of what in the event of the marriage going pear-shaped. On the other hand, if both husband and wife prosper and accumulate significant amounts of loot or property during the course of their marriage, and then decide to split, protracted legal arguments are liable to chip the gilt off the gingerbread for both parties. For a young, professional couple, a simple pre-nup anticipating certain possibilities may be worth the premium.

THE 'BLACKENING' RITUAL

Scottish weddings have traditional rituals of their own. Very often the groom has his stag night on the eve of the wedding, but in Scotland he tends to be costumed in Highland clothes and paraded about the town with a great deal of noisy banter. The groom can anticipate with a certain gloomy resignation, that at the end of the evening he will be stripped, covered in treacle and soot and tied to a tree for the night. This is called the 'blackening'. Presumably, it is a warning to him that on becoming a pillar of married respectability, it will not be in his best interests to get ideas above his station.

Meanwhile, in her kitchen, the bride's feet will be plunged into a tub full of opaque, soapy water. Into the tub there will have been placed a wedding ring belonging to one of the older women in the family. Now, the bride's companions will ritually wash her feet. Members of the stag party may wander by, leer in and try to get a peep at her. Such distractions she must ignore.

At the end of the washing ceremony, the bride will be lifted into and held down in the tub where she will be smothered in treacle and soot – both the groom and the bride have now been suitably 'blackened'. Then there is a scrabble for the ring hidden in the water. Romantically minded young ladies cherish the belief that whoever retrieves the ring will be the next in line to walk down the aisle.

MARRY AND LIVE LONGER

Researchers from Duke University Medical Center in the US published their findings of a study of married couples in the *Annals of Behavioral Medicine* journal in 2013. Having analysed data from nearly 5,000 people, they came to the conclusion that middle-aged people without a spouse or a partner are at a greater risk of dying prematurely than those who are married.

It is thought that the emotional and functional support a couple give each other are important to bolster the desire to battle on with their lives. It also suggests that a man can increase the chances of a longer life if his bride is between 15 and 17 years his junior. Why this should be is best left to the imagination.

NUNS

Those devout women who decide to become nuns must take three vows:

1. A vow of poverty
2. A vow of obedience
3. A vow of celibacy

Celibacy is not the same as virginity, so it is therefore possible for a divorced woman to join the sisterhood. It is equally possible for a sister who has renounced her vows to go back into the world and become a married woman.

During the ceremony to become a nun, the following words are spoken or, depending on the Order, an approximation of the same: 'Receive this ring, for you are betrothed to the Eternal King; keep faith with your bridegroom so that you may come to the wedding feast of eternal joy.' (Edward Foley, *Rites of Religious Profession*, 1989.)

At another point in the ordination, the nun will say, 'My Lord Jesus Christ has betrothed me with this ring; and adorned me as his spouse.'

It follows that a woman, while she remains in her chosen Order as a nun, cannot marry a man (see Brides of Christ, page 131).

Chapter 4
Doing it

WEDDING BELLS

Whenever there is a church wedding, campanologists rejoice and get ready for a big pull. The ringing of bells before the ceremony and after the deed is done is considered a jubilant experience.

Originally, the ringing of bells at a wedding amidst a general cacophony were the means by which the Celts scared off evil spirits intent on harming the bride and groom. Mother Nature held a lot of mystery and terror for the Celts, who warded off unpredictable danger in the only way they could – by screaming and making as much noise as possible in an attempt to scare the pants off it. The bells are also a reminder for tardier participants to get to the church on time. Now that civil ceremonies at registry offices are on the increase, the joyous peel of wedding bells is becoming something of a rarity.

The Americans have started a tradition of their own. They take small hand bells to a wedding, particularly if one of the parents of the couple is too ill to attend or has passed away. At the start of the ceremony, a special bell is placed on a table. The officiator will ask the bride or the groom to fetch the bell. There is a special reading in honour of the missing loved one, after which the bride (or groom) will ring the bell three times.

The custom of the bell ringer greeting the bride on her arrival seldom occurs any more. Traditionally, Scots used to engage a bagpiper to escort the bride on her arrival, but it is more common now to follow the old Irish tradition in which she is 'rung in' by the bell ringer – or ringers. The ringer walks down the aisle preceding the bride. Often, the guests are given hand bells so that they may join in the ring-a-ding-a-ling. The bells ring out again at the end of the ceremony, at which point the couple kisses. These 'kissing bells' are taken home by the newly-weds. Should they ever have an argument (God forbid!), one of them is supposed to pick up the little bell and ring it as a reminder of what was said in their marriage vows and how much they love each other. Sometimes it works. But not always.

The move from church to civil ceremonies doesn't mean that church bells can no longer be used. Hand-bell ringers can be hired. It is even possible to hire a portable unit of nine bronze church bells that can 'ring the changes' according to the couple's requirements.

A Grade II-listed building, the Whitechapel Bell Foundry, is the oldest manufacturer of bells in the world. It was established during the reign of Elizabeth I in 1570. In fact, the foundry was developed from an even earlier establishment on an adjacent site created by Master Founder Robert Chamberlain during the reign of Henry V in1420. During the Second World War, the original 'White Chapel', the Church of St Mary – just a few hundred feet away from the foundry – was destroyed by a bomb.

Bells made in Whitechapel are exported all over the world. The foundry casts large bells for change-ringing peals in church towers, single tolling bells and carillon bells, as well as their complete range of accessories.

WEDDING DRESSES

Anne of Brittany was crowned Queen of France on 8 February 1492. Just over six years later, her husband Charles died, and by the terms of her marriage she had to marry Charles's successor, Louis XII. This was complicated by the fact that Louis XII was already married. He had to crave an annulment from the Pope, Alexander VI, who happened to be a Borgia, (which must have been a relief since he was easy to bribe).

Apart from remaining Queen of France, Anne acquired fresh titles and privileges all over the continent. By way of celebration, at her wedding in January 1499, she wore a white dress. This innovative act was the beginning of the Western custom for brides to wear white for their weddings.. Before that, white clothes had been associated with death; bodies were wrapped in white shrouds.

In Britain, gold and silver wedding dresses did not go out of fashion entirely until Queen Victoria married Prince Albert of Saxe-Coburg, in 1840. Victoria's breathtaking white satin gown caught the public's imagination, and the style set by Victoria's couturiers has lasted until the present day. Curiously, as she lay dying 61 years later, Victoria left instructions that she was to be buried wearing her white wedding veil. Could she have nursed some secret hope that she would be rejoined with her beloved Albert? For someone who had spent so much of her life in mourning, it was curious that she claimed to detest the trend for dressing in black for funerals.

The fashion for the 'white wedding' was compounded in France when Empress Eugénie married Napoleon III in 1853 in a white fairy-tale gown that was elaborately em-broidered. Then in 1858, when Queen Victoria's eldest daughter, the Princess Royal, wore a complicated confection of white moiré antique and Honiton lace, with floral details, extravagant white wedding dresses had arrived and were here to stay.

Godey's *Lady's Book* (one of the most influential monthly

magazines for women in 19th-century America, founded by Louis Antoine Godey), contained the following statement in an 1849 edition: 'Custom has decided, from the earliest ages, that white is the most fitting hue, whatever may be the material. It is the emblem of the purity and innocence of girlhood, and the unsullied heart she now yields to the chosen one.' To this day, girls prefer to choose white, but how many are virgins is debatable.

It is considered unlucky for the bride to make her own dress; and it is traditional that some small part – a thread, a bow, whatever – must be left off until the actual moment she leaves her house to go to the church. Superstition also has it that all the pins must be removed from the wedding dress. Should even one pin remain, it is said the bride is doomed to have bad luck.

With regard to the suitability of the colour chosen for the wedding dress, here is an old poem (there are several variations) to serve as a reminder:

Married in white, you will have chosen right.
Married in grey, you will go far away.
Married in black you will wish yourself back.
Married in red you will wish yourself dead.
Married in blue, you will always be true.
Married in pearl, you'll live in a whirl.
Married in green, ashamed to be seen.
Married in yellow, ashamed of the fellow.
Married in brown, you'll live out of town.
Married in pink, your spirits will sink.

Honestly, you couldn't make these things up.

Following the outbreak of the First World War austerity

swept across the world and dresses in general became more utilitarian. Among the first garments to be dispensed with were tightly laced corsets, while wedding dresses also became much simpler.Coco Chanel exerted her influence on the Roaring Twenties by designing shorter wedding dresses with longer trains of lace, then when the Second World War came along, the cash-strapped couple was often forced to go through the matrimonial motions without a wedding dress at all. It became established practice for military personnel, male and female, to get married in their dress uniforms.

World's longest wedding dresses

The contender for the longest wedding dress to date was made from 1.86 miles (nearly 3 km) of tulle bordered by 6 miles (9.65 km) of silk. It was worn by Elena de Angelis for her wedding in Casal di Princice (outside Naples, Italy) in September, 2011.

However, the *Guinness World Records* claims that the longest wedding dress train was designed by the Andree Salon fashion house and displayed at the Wedding Fair in Bucharest in March 2012. It was nearly 3 km (1.85 miles) long. It used 4,700 metres of taffeta, 5.5 metres of Chantilly lace, 45 metres of lining, 1,857 sewing needles and 150 spool threads.

Princess Diana's wedding dress

Princess Diana's wedding dress, designed by Elizabeth and David Emanuel, was valued at £9,000. It was described as a 'puffball meringue wedding dress' with puffed sleeves and a frilly neckline. The dress was made of silk taffeta and decorated with lace, sequins and 10,000 pearls. The wedding took place on 29 July 1981.

The Duchess of Cambridge's wedding dress

The Duchess of Cambridge's wedding dress had a lace appliqué bodice using an old Irish technique called 'Carrickmacross'. It involved intricate detailing of roses for England, thistles for Scotland, daffodils for Wales and shamrocks for Ireland applied to ivory silk tulle. The wedding of Prince William and Catherine Middleton took place on 29 April 2011. Sarah Burton received an OBE for her highly admired design.

Queen Victoria's Wedding Dress

Queen Victoria's dress was of rich white satin and trimmed with orange flower blossoms. A veil of Honiton lace, valued then at £1,000 (a fantastic sum of many tens of thousands of pounds nowadays), covered a headdress made up on a wreath of orange flower blossoms. The satin, which was of a pure white, was manufactured in Spitalfields. Queen Victoria wore the star of the Order of the Garter and an armlet inscribed with the order's motto: '*Honi soit qui mal y pense*' ('shame on him who thinks evil of it'). The lace of Victoria's bridal dress, though popularly called Honiton lace, was actually created in the village of Beer, about ten miles from Honiton. Two hundred seamstresses took nine months to assemble it.

The lace forming the flounce of the dress measured four yards, and was three quarters of a yard in depth. The veil, which was one and a half yards square, gave employment to lace makers for six weeks. The Queen kept the veil in safekeeping for her funeral. The wedding took place on 10 February 1840. In order that Victoria's dress should be unique, all designs for the garment were subsequently destroyed.

Queen Elizabeth II's wedding dress

Elizabeth II was already married when she acceded to the throne in 1952. Her wedding to the Duke of Edinburgh took place in November 1947. In Britain at the time, severe austerity measures were still in place following the Second World War. Silkworms had to be imported to make the dress, but the so-called 'enemy silkworms' of Japan and Italy could not be used. Fortunately, friendly silkworms were eventually obtained from Nationalist China.

Princess Elizabeth's ivory silk wedding dress was designed by the Court Designer, Norman Hartnell. Her star-patterned bridal train was 4 metres (13 feet) in length. Rumour had it that the design had been inspired by a 1482 painting called *Primavera* by Botticelli. A diamond-fringe tiara secured the tulle veil. Ten thousand seed pearls, imported from America, were sewn onto the dress, which was 'skilfully worked in pearl and diamante, combined with flowing lines of wheat ears, the symbol of fertility'. It seemed to work, as the Queen went on to have four children.

FLORAL BRIDAL CROWNS

In ancient times, the bride wore a crown (sometimes called a chaplet), for her marriage nuptials. This would originally have been woven from reeds rather than, as became fashionable later, myrtle or roses. A crown wreath into which orange blossoms are woven is said to be an idea invented by the Saracens and brought back by the Crusaders. If this folk memory is true, the floral chaplet has been around since the 13th century. It has gone in and out of fashion several times.

In Jewish marriages the bride is often called 'Princess' and the groom used to be regarded as a king for the day and would wear a crown. The custom of a bridal crown with or without a veil is a tradition that is kept up in Sweden, where in its original form it used to be called *piglocken* or *huvudla.* If a bride decides against wearing a bridal crown, she runs the risk of being severely teased.

WEDDING MARCHES

Wedding marches are popular for both church and civil ceremonies. As the procession enters the church, the most commonly played march is the 'Bridal Chorus' from Richard Wagner's opera *Lohengrin* (first performed in 1850). At the finish, for the grand exit down the aisle, it has become almost de rigueur to play 'The Wedding March' by Felix Mendelssohn (1842), who wrote it as incidental music for Shakespeare's *A Midsummer Night's Dream.*Other marches often chosen for weddings include the following:

Beethoven's 'Ode to Joy'
Mouret's 'Rondeau'
Bach's 'Jesu, Joy of Man's Desiring'
Jeremiah Clarke's 'Trumpet Voluntary'
(properly, 'The Prince of Denmark's March', and often misattributed to Purcell)
Handel's 'Water Music Suite – Finale'

'Here Comes the Bride'

These are the lyrics to Richard Wagner's 'Bridal Chorus':

Here comes the bride
Dressed all in light;
Radiant and lovely
She shines in his sight.
Gently she slides

Graceful as a dove,
Meeting her bridegroom,
Her eyes full of love.
Long have they waited,
Long have they planned.
Life goes before them
Now hand in hand.
Asking God's blessing
As they begin
Life with new meaning
Life shared as one.
Entering God's union
Bowed before his throne –
Promising each other
To have and to hold.

Irreverent youngsters have been known to sing, 'Here comes the bride, 50 inches wide…' Say no more.

GIVING AWAY THE BRIDE

When a woman is given away on her wedding day, a reliable male friend, usually her father, will lead her towards the man she is to marry.

Until recent times, it was invariably the case that daughters were considered to be the property of their fathers. When the girl reached nubile age, and a young man wanted to wed her, he would formally ask her father for his daughter's hand in marriage. This formality, polite as it seemed, was the more sophisticated method of one man challenging the alpha male for a change in ownership.

In Western countries, with the emancipation of women, a degree of independence has developed. Today, a woman decides for herself whether she wants to become somebody's wife and take on the responsibilities of married life. After a proposal of marriage, she may, if she wishes, eliminate her father from any part of the equation. There is growing acquiescence that a bride may choose to walk alone down the aisle. Women have also gained independence and enough confidence to resent having to use the words, 'promise to honour and obey', in the ceremony. It has become increasingly common for a bride and groom to write their own set of conditions by which to abide.

Exceptionally rich and privileged people still negotiate a dowry but, in general, the prospective groom no longer pays a price to gain his bride. An engagement ring will clinch the agreement.

PORCH WEDDINGS

In England, wedding ceremonies did not take place inside churches until 1563. Until then, marriages were conducted outside the front doors of the church, in the porch – the place where proclamations and public announcements were commonly made. It was not until the ceremony was over that the wedding party would troop into the church for prayers. (Few churches had pews in those days.)

A series of events resulting from decisions on high led to change. Henry VIII's chief minister, Thomas Cromwell (*c.* 1485–1540), ordered parish churches to make a permanent record of all births, marriages and deaths (1538). Then, during the short reign of Edward VI (1546–53) there was a popular revolt in the west of England against the Prayer Book. A new *Protestant Book of Common Prayer* (1549) was distributed, translating the old Latin liturgies with slightly deviant texts into English. What's more, religious processions were banned; Catholics were furious and rose up in arms, but the authorities in London were not to be thwarted and they tasked a Protestant archdeacon named William Body with destroying Catholic religious imagery. In areas where Catholic loyalty still prevailed, such as Devon and Cornwall, there was outrage and the peasants revolted. William Body was murdered and the turmoil that followed became known as the 'Prayer Book Rebellion'. An army was assembled and sent to squash the uprising. During the many ensuing skirmishes and battles, more than 5,500 Catholics were killed. This spurred the authorities into accelerating religious reforms until a new Protestant uniformity prevailed.

For Catholics, now a subdued minority, the Council of Trent (1563, see Appendix 1) ruled that the marriage ritual is a Blessed Sacrament and must take place in the presence of Jesus Christ. From that time on, weddings, whether Catholic or Protestant, moved off the porch and into the church itself. After the Hardwicke Marriage Act (1754), a ceremony became a legal requirement in England and Wales.

POSH WEDDINGS

When Donald Trump married his third wife, Melania Knauss, in 2005, the reception was held at his 18-acre Mar-a-Lago Club in Palm Beach, Florida. Forty-five chefs were employed and, as well as preparing the banquet, they produced a Grand Marnier wedding cake weighing 90 kg (200 lbs). The venue was filled with 10,000 flowers. Melania's wedding dress weighed 27 kg (60 lbs) and was decorated with 1,500 rhinestones.

Lavish as this was, it didn't trump a wedding that had taken place the previous year. Steel baron Lakshmi Mittal, the world's fifth richest man, lavished $60 million (£36 million) on the wedding of his daughter Vanisha to Amit Bhatia in 2004. As an example of the 'no expenses spared' policy, the invitations, which were 20 pages long, were delivered by hand in silver boxes. The wine alone was reported to have cost more than $1,500,000 (£900,000). The nuptials lasted for five nights in Paris before moving on to Versailles and the 1,000 guests were accommodated in five-star hotels.

The most extravagant ever, according to the *Guinness World Records*, is claimed to be the 1981 wedding of Sheikh Mohammed bin Rashid Al Maktoum, who is the current ruler of Dubai. A special stadium was built to accommodate the 20,000 guests; the nuptials lasted seven days. Its total estimated cost was $44,500,000, which in today's terms would exceed $100 million (£60 million).

WEDDING RINGS

The bride wears her wedding ring on the third finger of her left hand as an outward display that she is spoken for. Appianus of Alexandria, the Roman historian (*c.* AD 150) described how the ancient Egyptians believed a delicate nerve runs from the third finger of the left hand to the heart (*vena amoris*), the thumb not being counted as a finger. This is not a view held by every culture, and certainly not by many anatomists.

In areas of India the ring is worn on the thumb. The Russians chiefly wear their wedding rings on the right hand. A bride brought up in the Greek Orthodox Church will wear the ring on her left hand before marriage and transfer it to her right hand afterwards.

When Christianity first came to England, a priest would take the bride's hand and place the ring first on her forefinger, saying, 'God the Father', then on the middle finger, saying 'God the Son', and finally on the third finger with, 'God the Holy Spirit', where it remained.

On the inside of the wedding ring there will often be engraved a line of poetry or a declaration of love.

It is not clear when the pledge ring for the wedding (the engagement ring) was deemed insufficient for the marriage. A wedding ring is a clearly visible sign to would-be admirers that the wearer is not just spoken for, but taken hook, line and sinker.

In Ireland, one of the most popular wedding rings is known as the Claddagh ring. Claddagh is a fishing village near Galway. The ring was first produced in the reign of Queen Mary II, (1662–94). The design of the Claddagh ring includes two hands clasping a crowned heart. The custom is for an engaged woman to wear the crown pointing inward and for a married woman to wear the crown pointing away from her body.

To produce enough gold for one wedding ring, the refining process uses 20 tons of waste material (according to mining expert Keith Slack).

Every year, an estimated 17 tons of gold is used to make wedding rings in the US. Engagement and wedding rings made of metal came into existence soon after the Greeks defeated the Egyptians in *c.* 333 BC. Rings of metal gradually replaced the circles of leather or papyrus prevalent up to that time.

It is considered to be a bad omen if the wedding ring is dropped at any time on the day of the ceremony.

Scottish gold and Celtic knot-work rings go back to the 16th century.

A gold wedding ring is supposed to have certain magical qualities. This chronicler recalls from his youth a wedding ring being rubbed on his eyelids as a cure for sties. Miraculously, this old wives tale, which recedes into the mists of time, actually seemed to work.

WEDDING BRACELETS

Traditions die, even in Ireland. It is no longer in vogue in that country for a romantically minded young man to present the object of his desire with a bracelet woven with human hair, partly his, partly hers, which was meant to represent the intertwining of their lives.

EARNEST MONEY

A throwback to those times of yore when a wedding was held less for the benefits of love and devotion and more for the exchange of contracts between two families, the definition of 'earnest money' in legal dictionaries is: 'A sum of money paid by a buyer at the time of entering a contract to indicate the intention of the buyer to carry out the contract.' According to prayer books of the 16th century, after the words, 'With this ring I thee wed' there followed the line, 'This gold and silver I give thee', at which point the 'earnest money' was paid. The bride was handed a leather purse containing gold and silver coins.

LUCKENBOOTH

In Scotland, a traditional brooch given to the bride on her wedding day is called a 'Luckenbooth'. Usually made of silver and engraved with two entwined hearts, the jewellery district of St Giles in Edinburgh sold them from 'luckenbooths' until about 200 years ago. Today, if one walks along the Royal Mile between Edinburgh Castle and the Palace of Holyroodhouse, one can still buy these brooches in the shops, together with all the accoutrements needed for a wedding. However, beautiful as the area is, it is not the cheapest place to shop.

When the first child is born, the Luckenbooth is pinned to the blanket for good luck.

THE KISS

The reason for the collision of lips at the end of a marriage ceremony may appear too obvious to need explanation. It's as traditional as a New Year's kiss in Times Square. Not widely known, however, is the fact that in olden days a kiss was the seal of an agreement – 'the clincher' – even between two men, hence the expression, 'sealed with a kiss'. Romantic and tender as it undoubtedly is, there is a half-forgotten but rational basis for 'the kiss'.

Incidentally, the clinking of wine glasses when two drinkers say 'cheers' – as frequently happens at weddings – has a similarly serious purpose. In ancient times, when a couple of sparring kings or lords met to parley, once the wine had been poured a little wine from each other's goblets was mixed in before they drank. That way, if one of them was trying to poison the other, they both died. This has echoed through the ages, leaving us today with a mere clinking of glasses before we toast each other's health. It is bad luck not to sip one's wine after clinking glasses.

THE BRIDAL BOUQUET

Bouquets and nosegays have something in common. In those centuries when plague decimated the population of Europe, a miasma of death and decay filled the air. Before sewage systems were laid down, the smell was, by all accounts, appalling. Everyone rode on horseback until late in the 16th century as coaches had not yet been invented. The streets were alive with filth and so people carried highly scented nosegays. Certain herbs, including rosemary, were believed to ward off plague and evil spirits. Wedding bouquets were barely distinguishable from these since they too were made up of herbs and spices and garlic – more for protection than decoration. In 1603 (the first year of King James I's reign), the price of rosemary rose from one shilling an armful to five shillings for a small bunch. This was an astronomical price for that era, but it is an indication of how much faith was put into nosegays as a plague preventer.

Over the past two hundred years, the bride's bouquet has gradually transformed into something of an art form. It has become fashionable to colour-coordinate the bouquet with the dresses of the bridesmaids.

Newly-weds in Hawaii wear garlands of flowers round their necks called leis. By all accounts, they are very good leis.

The tossing of the bridal bouquet following the marriage ceremony is the modern-day equivalent of throwing the torch in ancient heathen ceremonies. The new wife must toss the bouquet backwards over her shoulder to be caught, hopefully, by one of the unmarried bridesmaids. Passing the warmth and light of the fireplace onto someone else implies that the proud possessor will soon become a new bride.

In North America, the bouquet is sometimes replaced by the bride's garter. It's all a question of whether the bride can get the garter off her leg or whether she needs help. Sometimes this can descend into raucous ribaldry.

THE BRIDAL VEIL

On the continent of Europe, there was once a custom for the bride's veil to be just transparent enough for her to see dimly where she was heading, but opaque enough from the outside that nobody could see in. The face hidden underneath was obscured to such an extent it could have belonged to any woman.

At the last moment, it was the groom's privilege to draw aside the veil to get a good look at her. If he had ever previously clapped eyes on his intended bride, he could now confirm that this was the woman of his choice.

The reason for this seemingly bizarre rigmarole goes back to the Biblical story of Jacob and Rachel. Jacob wanted to marry Rachel so he asked her father, Laban. Laban agreed, with the proviso that Jacob must first labour in his fields for seven years. Jacob took a deep breath, rolled up his sleeves and set off to look after Laban's sheep and cattle.

Seven years later, presumably calloused but still determined, Jacob got the wedding he'd been waiting for. As was the tradition, the bride wore a heavy veil. It was only the following morning that Jacob got a good look at his wife's face and realised that he had been quite literally hoodwinked. His new wife was Rachel's older sister, Leah. In those Old Testament times, it was traditional for the eldest sister to be married off before the younger sisters were allowed that opportunity.

Having laboured in the fields for seven years for no pay and ending up with the wrong woman, Jacob was understandably a tad disgruntled. He decided to have stern words with his duplicitous father-in-law. Responding to Jacob's complaint, Laban mumbled an excuse to the effect of, 'Oh, sorry, Jacob. Didn't think you'd notice. But if you really want to marry Rachel, you may do so, as long as you labour in my fields for another seven years.' To know how this story ends, read Genesis, chapters 29 and 30.

This tale illustrates how the need came about for a groom

to unveil his bride: he had to make sure of her true identity before committing himself to his final vows. In an arranged marriage (in which case he may never have seen her before), the groom probably wouldn't recognise the woman underneath the veil anyway. In such circumstances, this removal of the veil presents him with an 11th-hour opportunity to abscond should the vision underneath the muslin prove so hideous that he cannot bear to countenance it on a regular basis till death do them part.

In England, following the Restoration, the bridal veil disappeared and did not make its way back into fashion until after Queen Victoria's wedding in 1840.

THE BRIDE STANDS ON THE LEFT

The reason that vehicles drive on the left on British roads is a hangover from the days of the coach and horses. Coaches started to become fashionable at the beginning of the 17th century and in those times all travelling men carried swords. Sitting on the right, the driver was able to unsheathe his sword with his right hand and wield it outside of the coach to defend himself.

The analogy holds true for a groom and his bride walking along the street or a church aisle. With the bride on his left, a right-handed man, if pressed, can fight more easily.

There was an age when men were only too eager to pick fights. In the English Houses of Parliament, the Government benches face the Opposition benches, but they are deliberately set apart from each other by a measurement that keeps them two sword lengths apart.

There always seems to be an exception that proves the rule. At certain military weddings in the United States it is the bride who will stand on the right of the groom. That country's inhabitants drive on the wrong side of the road too.

LAWFULLY JOINED TOGETHER

At the moment of truth, the Minister says words to this effect:

> Dearly beloved, we are gathered together here in the sight of God to join together this Man and this Woman in Holy Matrimony; which is an honourable estate, instituted of God in Paradise, and into which Holy estate these two persons present come now to be joined. Therefore if any man can show any just cause why they may not lawfully be joined together, let him now speak, or else hereafter forever hold his peace.

This is the point of no return. The man and woman may then exchange vows and rings and be pronounced man and wife.

In the novel *Jane Eyre* by Charlotte Bronte there is a famous moment when Mr. Rochester is at the altar about to be married…

> …'Wilt thou have this woman for thy wedded wife?' – then a distinct and near voice said:'The marriage cannot go on: I declare the existence of an impediment.'
>
> The clergyman looked up at the speaker, and stood mute; the clerk did the same; Mr. Rochester moved slightly, as if an earthquake had rolled under his feet: taking a firmer footing, and not turning his head or eyes, he said, 'Proceed.'
>
> Profound silence fell when he had uttered that word, with deep but low intonation. Presently Mr. Wood said:

'I cannot proceed without some investigation into what has been asserted, and evidence of its truth or falsehood.'

'The ceremony is quite broken off,' subjoined the voice behind us. 'I am in a condition to prove my allegation: an insuperable impediment to the marriage exists.' ...Mr. Wood seemed at a loss.

'What is the nature of the impediment?' he asked. 'Perhaps it may be got over – explained anyway.'

'Hardly,' was the answer: 'I have called it insuperable, and I speak advisedly.'

The speaker came forwards, and leaned on the rails. He continued, uttering each word distinctly, calmly, steadily, but not loudly.

'It simply consists in the existence of a previous marriage. Mr. Rochester has a wife now living.'

My nerves vibrated to those low-spoken words as they had never vibrated to thunder – my blood felt their subtle violence as it had never felt frost or fire: but I was collected, and in no danger of swooning. I looked at Mr. Rochester: I made him look at me. His whole face was colourless rock: his eye was both spark and flint.'...

It's a good book and at this juncture there are still 170 pages to go.

FATHER OF THE BRIDE

That glazed look you detect in the eyes of the bride's father at a wedding is caused by his subconscious accounting system tapping away at a calculating machine. After he's given away his daughter, the father of the bride is, of course, as useless as a spare cake at a wedding. Now that his bank account has been severely depleted his task is done. All that is left for him to do is to favour his daughter with a broad smile before turning to his wife with the hint of a tear in his eye.

Once the fruit of his loins has been commandeered by another man, it is his duty to make the first speech at the reception. It should be extremely short. In fact, if it is written on the back of more than one cheque book it is too long. Anecdotes about how his daughter wet her drawers at the age of four are not to be recommended.

After pausing for an appropriate length of time to let the ovation die down, he must remain swaying on his feet long enough to toast the happy couple.

Being careful to show no rancour as he catches the eye of the groom, he should resume his seat and shut up for the rest of the evening until his wife begs him, with a steely glance, to drive her home if he is sober enough. In response to this implied insinuation that he has been at the sherry, he cannot allow a look of premeditated cunning despoil his features. An astute 'Father of the bride' will have played his cards close to his chest and the best man will have arranged a chauffeur-driven limo, or at the very least, a taxi, to be on standby. After all, it is probably the father of the bride who has paid for the whole shebang.

Before he weaves towards the waiting vehicle, he should stiffen the upper lip in a rictus grin, pose for photographs, and keep his hands well away from the matron of honour.

MOTHER OF THE BRIDE

The bride's mother is expected to show how happy she is by shedding tears at unexpected moments. It is assumed that this weeping is caused by her sadness at losing a daughter. There is always the possibility that they may indicate her relief at getting the spare bedroom back.

THE WEDDING CAKE

Fire, food, cooking – these are all ancient domestic elements associated with weddings. For marriage ceremonies, the Romans made cakes out of a mixture of flour, salt and water. It is easy to imagine these pasties were not particularly tasty, which is the likely reason why they were eventually crumbled up and chucked over the heads of the lucky couple.

After King Charles I had his head chopped off, Oliver Cromwell took control. Not known for his love of fun and games, Cromwell banned Bishops, closed theatres and got rid of most of the church rituals. It was only when Charles II was restored to the English throne in 1660 that maypoles, dancing and weddings were allowed to flourish again. Cakes came into fashion in a more spectacular fashion than they had ever been.

Before the interregnum, the cakes made for weddings had been pathetic offerings, consisting mainly of piles of biscuits and scones. When you read the list of ingredients – sugar, eggs, milk, flour, currants and spices – these must have looked and tasted a lot like hot cross buns, but without being hot, without the cross, and without being particularly bunny.

When the English monarchy was restored, chefs were shipped in from France and all over the continent. Suddenly, pastry cooking was on the up. It was almost worth getting married to get your teeth into the new iced wedding cakes alone. The Great Fire of London in 1666 started in a bakery near Ludgate Circus, in aptly named Pudding Lane. Perhaps they were experimenting with wedding cakes? On Tuesday, 4 September 1666, two days after the fire broke out, the nearby church of St Bride's, a site of Christian worship since the Romans left, burnt to the ground. Altogether 87 churches went up in smoke in the space of three days.

(A brief digression on the name: for more than 1,500 years, marriages have been taking place at St Bride's Church, even though the name has no particular relevance to 'brides'. Legend has it that the church was founded in about AD 480 by a saint hailing from Ireland, where she was known as St Brigid. One may surmise that Cockneys couldn't get their tongues round 'St Brigid' and called her 'St Bride' for short.)

Following the Great Fire, Christopher Wren rebuilt St Bride's. It was reopened in 1678, but the steeple was not completed according to Wren's original design and it took five more years of fund-raising to add all five octagonal tiers. When it was finished, the City of London bakers looked at it and decided that a wedding cake would look a tasty treat indeed if it were to be modelled on the structure of the church. (Or was it the other way round? Is it too fanciful to suppose that French pastry chefs, with their limited command of the English language, actually thought that St Bride's was designed to look like a wedding cake?)

Five-tiered cakes were tried but proved just a bit too wobbly. Three-tiered wedding cakes seemed to hold together quite well and became much in demand. However, the tall structure of the cake demanded it be cut with a steady hand to avoid an architectural disaster.

Today, it has become part of the tradition for the bride and groom to take joint responsibility for the cake's stability. You'll notice that the newly-weds always display a becoming hesitancy as they approach the cake together with the intention of cutting it. The bride holds the knife in her right hand and places the tip of the knife at the centre of the bottom tier. The groom places his right hand on her right hand. She places her left hand on his right hand. Then they gingerly make an incision in the cake. The onlookers smile approvingly and nod wisely, believing they can appreciate the symbolism of it all. The first slice of cake is shared between the happy couple.

Bridesmaids are supposed to take their slice home and tuck it under the bed pillows. They are assured that this will evoke images of their future husbands. Traditionally, the top tier of the cake is preserved to celebrate the birth of the couple's first child.

BRIDAL ALE

In medieval times a special ale was brewed for weddings called *byrd ealu* – 'bride's ale'. This became corrupted through the years to 'bridal', a word that was originally associated with 'wedding feast'. In effect, the word 'booze-up' is a corruption of the medieval word, 'bridal'.

THE WEDDING CANDLE

The wedding feast and toast directly descend from the wedding Eucharist ceremony where the couple toast each other from the cup of love and eat from the bread of life and health. The wedding, or unity, candle is a relatively recent addition to wedding celebrations, and is especially popular in the USA. The candle burns with three flames that merge towards the central wick. The middle candle represents the new family. When it is joined by the bride's candle and the groom's candle, the side tapers are blown out and the candle of the new family remains.

GARTER TOSSING

Apparently, the tossing the garter tradition stems from the rituals of 14th-century England. The superstitious people of that time believed that a piece of a bride's wedding dress would bestow good luck. No sooner was the ceremony over than the unmarried guests would begin pulling at the bride's dress and ripping it to tatters. To play for time, and to hold them off, the bride threw her garters into the mob.

As the years passed, this evolved into the current custom where the groom tastefully removes his bride's garter from her leg and throws it into the crowd of baying guests. Some observers see this as a symbolic act of the bride's deflowering.

There is a widely held superstition that if the bouquet strikes the recipient 'on the nose' the lucky young lady will be the next up for marriage. Then there's a follow-through – if the man who catches the garter 'on the nose' gives it to the lady who caught the bouquet, who can tell where that will lead? Probably to the next dance... But are they going to end up at his place or hers?

BRIDESMAIDS

The duty of the chief bridesmaid (or, if she is married, the matron or maid of honour) is to give the bride moral and practical support. As soon as the marriage is announced, the chief bridesmaid and the best man get together to form a channel of communication between the two families during the preparations. She will help to select the wedding dress, make arrangements for the hen night, give advice on the choice of bridesmaids and pageboys and, if a decision is made to follow the American tradition, organise the bridal shower. It is the job of the other bridesmaids to assist her, and to support the bride during the ceremony and at the reception afterwards.

In medieval times the bridesmaids' role was to work with the groom's men to protect the couple. Bridesmaids were dressed up in clothes similar to the bride in order to confuse evil spirits who might have had reason to sabotage the ceremony. The bridesmaids formed a posse round the bridegroom and led him into the church. The best men, meanwhile, escorted the bride to the altar. Over the years, as society has become less overtly violent, the roles became what we are accustomed to today.

In the bride's entourage, the maid of honour will act as one of the witnesses. She will also assist with the invitations that need to be sent out at least two months before the big day. She will probably purchase a 'guest book', which the bride will cherish as a keepsake, as a record containing the signatures of everyone present at the wedding.

Royal weddings tend not to stint on the number of bridesmaids. In 1947, Princess Elizabeth (as she was at the time) had eight bridesmaids, most of them younger than the 21-year-old bride. In July 1981, Princess Diana had five bridesmaids, the youngest of whom was five. In 2011, Royal bride Kate Middleton, now the Duchess of Cambridge, invited her husband-to-be's goddaughter as well as Camilla Parker Bowles' granddaughter, both aged three, to do the honours. If this trend continues, it is entirely possible that at the next Royal wedding, one of the bridesmaids could be a babe-in-arms.

PAGEBOYS AND USHERS

In large families, it is not unusual for the bride to delegate certain responsibilities to her younger brothers or nephews. This can be good psychology. It gives them something to concentrate on and keeps them out of mischief. They can help to lift the train of her dress or carry the rings on a cushion.

Until the 18th century, the bride was escorted to church

by two bride's men. Later, during the 19th century, these were replaced by pageboys.

Ushers are like traffic cops. They organise the parking, show guests to their seats in church, check that glasses are topped up and guide the guests to and from the ceremony.

PENNY WEDDINGS OR 'BRIDEWAIN'

In the 19th and the early part of the 20th centuries, many of those in the working class could only legitimately take time off work at Christmas and Easter. As they had next to no money to pay church fees, it was quite common to conduct multiple weddings simultaneously. The collection of couples would stand together and recite the words of the service in unison, except for when it came to their individual vows: 'I – [name] – take thee – [name] – to be my lawful wedded …' et cetera. On completion of the ceremony, each couple contributed one penny to make up the fee – hence the term. It was said that the record for marrying the most couples at the same time in England was held by a curate in Worcester – 26 simultaneous weddings on a Christmas Day.

Penny weddings used to be called 'bridewains'. Wain is an old English word for cart (as in haywain); a bridewain was the vehicle that brought the gifts to the bride.

Penny weddings were once traditional in Scotland. Guests were expected to bring their own food and drink to the celebrations after the ceremony. Sir David Wilkie, the Scottish painter, famously depicted *The Penny Wedding* in 1818. It was painted for George IV.

But the Welsh had an even more elaborate version, later transported to the US (see Biddings below).

BIDDINGS

Of Welsh origin, a bidding letter is really no more than an invitation card to a wedding, usually beautifully decorated. However, a whole tradition has sprung from this ancient custom.

The Bidder (in Welsh *Gwahoddwr)* is a person delegated to invite the guests. This chap dresses up rather like an old-fashioned beadle or town crier. He carries a staff of office, a wand made of willow stripped of its bark and decorated with gaily-coloured ribbons. Where he would ordinarily sport a boutonnière, he attaches instead a white lover's knot. Ribbons flow from his hat. He looks perfectly lovely. Dressed thus, his task is to call round to the houses of all the people to be invited to the wedding. At each house, he strikes the floor with his staff and formally announces the date of the proposed marriage.

It is now the duty of the guests to contribute voluntarily towards 'the purse and girdle', (*pwrs a gwregys*). As the wedding day nears, the wedding gifts (*ystafell*) are delivered to the home of the bride. These consist mostly of household articles such as pillows, blankets and cutlery. But there is also a monetary element, which the bride-to-be tucks into her girdle for a rainy day. Meanwhile, back in his house, her fiancé is busy receiving other sorts of gifts. In farming communities, for example, these presents may well include chickens, ducks and scythes and the such.

The gifts would be meticulously recorded so that they could be suitably reciprocated when the time came.

BESOM WEDDINGS

A besom is an old-fashioned broom shaped like the traditional witch's broomstick. Besom weddings were a temporary arrangement meant to last just one year and a day. The practice spread from Wales across Europe and Africa and became a form of ceremony favoured by African-American slaves on the plantations of the New World.

A besom was laid across the floor of the threshold of a door. This door would lead into the home or hut where nuptial arrangements had been anticipated. Witnesses were called in to observe the couple as they jumped over the besom and into the house without touching the broom or the doorframe. After a year and a day, if everything was sweetness and light, they could legitimise their marriage in a formal manner. On the other hand, should things have not worked out as hoped, they could annul the arrangement by leaping backwards out of the house, over the besom and into the street outside.

WHY ALMONDS?

Five sugar-coated almonds represent health, wealth, happiness, fertility and longevity (see Wedding favours, page 59).

The Roman poet, Ovid, gave us a myth in which Demophon, while in Thrace, fell in love with Phyllis. The marriage was postponed because Demophon had to go back home to attend his father's funeral. He promised to return within a month but was seriously delayed. Phyllis despaired and, assuming she had been left in the lurch, killed herself. The gods took pity on her and turned her into an almond tree. On his return, Demophon was grief-stricken. His conjugal rights had gone out of the window. He made a sacrifice to the almond tree, declaring his eternal love. The gods were moved by this and so caused the almond tree to burst into blossom and embrace him. Based on this myth, the almond has become a symbol of undying love.

GUARD OF HONOUR

After a man and a woman have come through the wedding ceremony unscathed, there may be other hurdles to face. To begin with there are the friends and friendly faces waiting outside. If the groom has an occupation requiring manual application, it may be reflected by a 'guard of honour' waiting for him as the pair leave the wedding venue. A military man might have swords held aloft forming an arch for the newlyweds to walk through, or any tools representative of the groom's trade. For policemen, expect truncheons. For car mechanics, exhaust pipes. Trombonists – well, you get the picture. In 1902, in Croydon, at a butcher's wedding, the couple were greeted by 'ringing the bells' on marrow bones and cleavers.

RIBBONS ON THE LIMO

Ribbons are draped in a V-shape over the bonnet (or 'the hood' as they prefer to say in the US) to identify a vehicle, likely to be a limo, as the wedding car among a possible convoy. Police will usually give it special dispensation.

Intricate bows made from ribbon are sometimes attached to the door handles. The ribbons are usually white (although purple and pink are becoming increasingly popular). They are cheap to buy and come in lengths of about 6 metres (20 ft) with a width of about 5 cm (2 in). If the limo is a hired vehicle, the duty driver will be an old hand at the game and adept at attaching these ribbons.

Chapter 5

Superstitions

CHIMNEY SWEEPS

Why are they supposed to bring luck to a wedding? The lyrics of Richard M. and Robert B. Sherman in the song 'Chim Chim Cher-ee' from their marvellous musical movie, *Mary Poppins*, perpetuated the custom, with its references to a sweep being 'as lucky as lucky can be', and that good luck will rub off if his hand is shaken, or he is blown a kiss.

In fact, this tradition is entrenched to such an extent in the public consciousness that even at the wedding of Elizabeth II to Prince Philip (in 1947, 17 years before *Mary Poppins* was released) a chimney sweep was hired and ushered into the Royal presence. Prince Philip, revered for his acerbic wit, was observed to warmly shake the chimney sweep's hand. It would have been interesting to hear what witty bon mot the Duke came up with later as he was wiping off the soot.

Anything connected with fire and the stove has always been associated with luck. It all boils down to those primary needs of food and warmth. A chimney sweep, whose whole life is spent in proximity to the hearth, is believed to carry good luck with him. By touching him, it was hoped that perhaps his luck would rub off on you.

Chimney sweeps first materialised in the 13th century when buildings began to incorporate chimneys that required fireplaces and hearths. Previously, homes had been heated with a centrally located open fire.

The traditional uniform of a chimney sweep was a black suit with shiny buttons and a black top hat. In the pantomime 'Cinderella' the character of Buttons probably originated as a young chimney sweep. Cinderella swept the cinders and bagged the soot.

The modern tradition of a chimney sweep deliberately turning up at weddings began nearly 250 years ago. The story goes that George III was riding in his carriage when a barking dog spooked his horses causing them to rear, threatening His Royal Personage with imminent disaster. By chance, a passing chimney sweep managed to calm the beasts and bring them under control. Then, without consideration of receiving any thanks or reward, the sweep continued cheerfully on his way. The king was deeply touched. (It should be pointed out that George III was not always entirely himself. Among many instances of his eccentricity, there was an occasion when he stopped his coach to get out and talk to a tree.)

Some time after the chimney sweep episode, when one of his six daughters was to be married (by a process of elimination this was probably Charlotte, the Princess Royal, who was married on 18 May 1797), George III sent out courtiers to scour the land for the unknown chimney sweep. When he was found, he was handed an invitation to attend the wedding in the belief that he would bring good luck with him. Many loving couples intent on tying the bonds of matrimony have followed the eccentric monarch's example ever since.

If the Princess concerned was poor Charlotte, then there is a bitter irony in all this – for the sweep's presence failed to bring much magic. Her marriage to Duke Frederick of Wurttemberg produced one child in 1798 – a stillborn daughter.

Now that coal fires are fast becoming something of a rarity, it is common practice to hire professional 'chimney sweeps' from specialist companies catering for weddings. It is alleged that today chimney sweeps gain more employment from attending weddings than they do from sweeping chimneys. Incidentally, the practice of sending small boys up chimneys was stopped in 1875, following a fatal accident at Fulbourn Hospital in Cambridgeshire.

The Chimney Sweeper

A poem by William Blake

When my mother died I was very young,
And my father sold me while yet my tongue
Could scarcely cry "'weep! 'weep! 'weep! 'weep!"
So your chimneys I sweep, & in soot I sleep.

There's little Tom Dacre, who cried when his head,
That curl'd like a lamb's back, was shav'd: so I said
"Hush, Tom! never mind it, for when you head's bare
You know that the soot cannot spoil your white hair."

And so he was quiet, & that very night,
As Tom was a-sleeping, he had such a sight!
That thousands of sweepers, Dick, Joe, Ned, & Jack,
Were all of them lock'd up in coffins of black.

And by came an Angel who had a bright key
And he open'd the coffins & set them free;
Then down a green plain leaping, laughing, they run,
And wash in a river, and shine in the Sun.

Then naked & white, all their bags left behind,
They rise upon clouds and sport in the wind;
And the Angel told Tom, if he'd be a good boy,
He'd have God for his father, & never want joy.

And so Tom awoke; and we rose in the dark,
And got with our bags & our brushes to work,
Tho the morning was cold, Tom was happy & warm,
So if all do their duty they need not fear harm.

THE MARRIAGE KNOT

In ancient Greece, brides would fasten their woollen girdles with a Herculean knot – a complicated knot that only the bridegroom was permitted to untie. As he did so, no doubt struggling with the darn thing, he made an oath to Juno that once it was undone he would follow the example of Hercules and his 13th Labour, whereby Hercules killed the Lion of Cithaeron as a favour for the King of Thespiae. His reward was the opportunity to make love to all 50 of the king's daughters in a single night. Hercules complied and they all bore sons.

That Hercules had stamina is beyond doubt. He had at least four wives and a number of boyfriends. At any rate, by the time the groom had managed to untie his bride's girdle, the odds are he was raring to go. It is unlikely that Hercules' record has ever been bested.

In later Roman times, the knot became a double knot with interlacing bows shaped like the figure eight. Written sideways, the figure eight represented the symbolic sign of infinity. Together with the wedding ring, this emphasised the intention to make an everlasting bond.

In the Hindu religion, the groom knots a ribbon round the neck of his bride. Before he finally tightens the knot, the bride's father can summarily dismiss the wedding. Once the ribbon is knotted into place, the marriage is a fait accompli.

TRUE LOVERS' KNOTS
(NODUS HERCULANUS)

The origin of the true lovers' knot goes back into the mists of antiquity. It began with the Delphic oracles whose divining wands had two serpents entwined around them. This evolved into the rod carried by the Greek god, Hermes.

In ancient Greece, brides used the same design as an interlocking 'knot' on their girdles, symbolising everlasting affection. In turn, the Roman messenger of the gods, Mercury, carried this symbol on his staff. Subsequently, Roman brides carried on the tradition with the *nodus Herculanus* wrought into their marriage girdles.

EROS/CUPID

In Greek mythology Eros is often depicted as a winged youth with a sylph-like figure, always at the ready with his bow and arrow to shoot darts at lovesick youths and maidens. The son of Aphrodite, he shoots the sting of love that inflames the heart.

The Romans adopted the Greek mythology and Eros became Cupid, the son of Venus. (In Latin *cupido* means desire.)

> Love looks not with the eyes, but with the mind,
> And therefore is winged Cupid painted blind.
> Nor hath love's mind of any judgement taste,
> Wings and no eyes figure unheedy haste,

And therefore is love said to be a child
Because in choice he is so oft beguiled.

(From *A Midsummer Night's Dream*
by William Shakespeare, *c.*1595)

TYING THE KNOT AND GETTING HITCHED

Nowadays, a couple might say to each other, 'Let's get hitched' or, 'It's time to tie the knot', and we know what they're getting at – that they're thinking of getting married. The expressions have come down to us from pagan times and neither refer strictly to marriage as we know it today.

'Tying the knot' used to be a legal way of marrying for just one year and one day, contracting a marriage on 1 May and ending it on 2 May the following year. Although a couple may live together as man and wife, it was originally meant to be a temporary arrangement. Some couples found themselves gritting their teeth until 2 May the following year. Neo-pagans of the 21st century still use the expressions, and sometimes perform the ceremony on 1 May.

'Getting hitched' referred to a form of marriage where no clergy were involved. Nonetheless, the ceremony, if witnessed, was considered a legally binding contract.

In Scotland, 'tying the knot' is said to have originated from the bride and the groom ripping their clan tartans and then tying the two strips together, symbolising the unity of both families. Hopefully, they did not get arrested for indecent exposure.

HANDFASTING

Utilised by the Catholic Church in the Middle Ages as a form of betrothal was a ceremony called 'Handfasting'. The word stems from the Old Norse *hand-festa* – meaning, 'to strike a bargain by joining hands'. To undergo this ceremony, a couple had their hands bound together using scarves or rope at the wrists. This, together with the Scottish tartan-tearing [see above], contributes to the genesis of the expression, 'Tying the knot'.

Handfasting was a legal form of marriage in Scotland until 1939. But the marriage was conditional on the couple enjoying togetherness for 13 moon cycles, after which, if they were agreeable, they could go through the ceremony again to extend their lives together for a further period. In some American states, it is still a legal form of cohabitation to this day.

One of the reasons the tradition has held on tenaciously in some outlying regions of the Western civilised world is because the Catholic Church's marriage reforms did not extend to those regions further away that were under Protestant influence, particularly those promulgated by the Council of Trent (see Appendix 1). The Celts, in particular, were unaffected by the Church of Rome. Generally speaking, 'handfasting' has been incorporated into the ceremony of 'engagement'.

In 1612, William Shakespeare (whose court appearances we know more about than his stage performances) found himself summoned as a witness in a court case. A few years prior to the case, William had been living in lodgings in Silver Street in the Cripplegate area of London. His landlords were Christopher and Marie Mountjoy – Huguenot tiremakers ('tire' being the vernacular form of 'attire' meaning 'head attire', they were, in fact, hatters). A marriage was arranged between the couple's daughter Mary and their apprentice, Stephen Belott. A substantial dowry of £60 had been promised by the betrothed girl's father to Stephen to allow him to set up as a 'tiremaker' on his own recognisance. The marriage took place in the form of a handfasting ceremony, which William Shakespeare witnessed.

However, the dowry was not forthcoming, and after a few years Stephen Belott took his parents-in-law to court. William Shakespeare was summoned as a witness. William claimed he could not remember much about it. The judge referred the case to arbitration by the church fathers of the French Church in London who awarded Belott a mere 20 nobles in settlement (£6 14s 4d in old money, but worth a great deal more today).

GOOD AND BAD OMENS

It is said to be unlucky for a bride to catch sight of herself in the mirror wearing her full wedding rig. Far-fetched as it seems, the reason for this belief is that she might leave behind part of herself in the reflection.

Similarly, tradition dictates that the groom should not see his bride before the ceremony. However, this is rooted in something more substantial. In the distant past, arranged marriages often resulted in the bride and groom never having seen each other (see Bridal veil, page 81). As the wedding day grew closer, both the man and the woman had high expectations of what their other half might look like. If, by accident, the groom did manage to get a glimpse of what he was in for, and if what he saw appalled him, he might do a runner before the off.

Any bride suffering from arachnophobia is unfortunate, because if she finds a spider in her wedding dress, she must not scream. Instead, it's best for her to consider it her lucky day. She can be equally ecstatic if she encounters a frog, a blind man, a black cat or a dove. Other things to look out for include lambs, rainbows and snow. (If it's a June wedding and it starts snowing, you are either an Eskimo or climate change has speeded up catastrophically.)

On the off chance that the blind man trips over the frog or the cat pounces on the dove, a bride's best recourse is to shut her eyes and make a beeline for the marriage venue. To top it all, she is entitled to hit the heights of ecstasy if an old grey mare canters past her. Old grey mares are a clincher for happy marriages – the older and the greyer the better.

While she continues on her journey, let us hope the bride does not come across a pig or a hare or an open grave. If she does, she is probably approaching the church from the wrong direction. Also, it's as well to avoid monks and nuns, since they too are portents of a barren relationship.

As for the groom, presuming him desirous of reassuring omens, there is a veritable menagerie for him to witness. These include goats, wolves and pigeons. Gladdened by the odd wolf or two, he may, while hurrying to get to the church on time, feel around for the loose change he doubtless remembered to shove in his pocket before leaving his bachelor abode. Then, if he spots some ghastly tramp weaving towards him, he can toss a coin in the smelly stranger's direction. The opportunity to toss pennies at smelly strangers is tremendously auspicious.

Meanwhile, the bride, on entering the church, must remember to step in with her right foot first. To set off on the wrong foot would be to invite disaster. The Romans were convinced that anything on a person's left side was guided by evil spirits. The Latin word *sinistra* means both 'left' and 'unlucky'. In the 21st century, it's attention to these little details that contribute to marital bliss. You can't be too careful.

It is supposed to be a bad omen for the church clock to strike during the ceremony.

The bride is tempting fate if she takes any part in the preparation of her own wedding cake. This is just as well, perhaps. If the cake turned out to be ghastly, the groom might get second thoughts then and there.

It was said that if a thunderstorm occurred during the wedding, the couple would remain childless.

If the wedding ring is dropped during the ceremony, it signifies that unspeakably ghastly things will happen.

Yes, in olden days they were not really happy unless they had something to worry about. Many of the clichéd traditions found in modern-day weddings stem from less-educated eras when even sophisticated people believed in hexes, sorcery and black magic. In addition, if there's a full moon, and it happens to be June, the worst is over and they're both in clover, and they are like mint to the lamb of even the worst lyricist.

HORSESHOES

There are a couple of reasons why the horseshoe is deemed to be lucky – particularly at weddings. Since the reasons are speculative, you can take your pick.

For the ancient Greeks, the crescent moon was associated with fertility, and the shape of a horseshoe seemed to them to be symbolic of the moon.

Another root goes back to about 940 in Glastonbury where St Dunstan resided and worked as a blacksmith. One day, he was asked to shoe a horse whose owner, the devout blacksmith was quick to perceive, was the Devil himself. Without further ado, St Dunstan burnt the shoe onto the hoof and hammered the nails in – but rather than onto the horse, he did so onto the cloven hoof of the Devil, who howled in anger and pain. St Dunstan made a bargain with the Devil: he agreed to alleviate the pain by removing the shoe if the Devil promised never to enter any house where a horseshoe hung above the door. The Devil signed an agreement and St Dunstan removed the nails. Thereafter, for several centuries – and even today, as it happens – Christian households, having been tipped the wink by St Dunstan, hung horseshoes above their doorways. The horseshoe is hung in a U-shape, with the curve at the bottom, so that the luck does not spill out.

Furthermore, at her wedding, a bride often had a 'lucky horseshoe' hanging from her shoulders held by ribbons, a tradition still sometimes seen today.

TYING SHOES TO THE GETAWAY CAR

There is a theory, not universally held, that the giving away of shoes after a marriage goes back to the ancient Egyptians. Apparently, against the backdrop of pyramids, an Egyptian father would hand over his daughter's sandals to the groom as a gesture to show that she was now the new husband's property. If this is so, one hopes the girl would have a second pair of sandals handy because standing on the hot sand on the outskirts of Cairo for any length of time would undoubtedly produce some nasty blisters.

As if this wasn't enough, some sources suggest that it was the custom to throw shoes at the newly-weds. Quite why this should become the practice has never been satisfactorily explained. Fortunately, the march of civilisation has replaced smelly old shoes with confetti, which is more difficult to clear up afterwards but less painful when it hits you.

Unfortunately, none of this really explains why shoes are tied to the back bumper of the car taking the couple away to a night of wedded bliss.

SLIPPERS AND THE 'UPPER HAND'

As well as the above practice, footwear had a slightly more sinister connotation. In another old English custom, the bride's father would give a pair of his old slippers (or in agricultural communities – his boots) to the groom. The underlying message behind this tradition was that the transfer of power had been well and truly handed over. The groom had been given entitlement to beat his wife with the slipper (or boot) if she displeased him. The slipper was positioned in a prominent place above the bed-head to remind the new bride that her husband had 'the upper hand'.

MONGOLIAN CHICKEN LIVERS

The Daur people are an ethnic minority living under the protection of China in Inner Mongolia. The word 'Daur' means cultivator and it is said they are the descendants of the brave Qidan tribe (916–1125). Many are shamanists, though a few are followers of Lamaism. With a population of less than 150,000, the Daur are bilingual but have no written language.

When a young Daurian lady takes a fancy to a man she will make an elaborate tobacco pouch and slip it into his pocket. Women marry when their age is an odd number, so most weddings take place when she is 17, 19 or 21 (the Chinese count the age of a person from conception not from the moment of parturition).

Chinese culture has influenced the Daur people regarding the date they marry. Astrologers are consulted to make sure that the sun and stars are in fortuitous alignment. The couple must marry on the half hour so that they begin their new life when the hands of the clock are moving upwards. And they uphold another odd tradition whereby the date of a wedding is determined by the state of a chicken liver. The prospective groom and his fiancée must use a knife to kill a chick and disembowel it. If the liver is good, they can set a date. If not, they have to wait awhile and try again. To Western sensibilities this begs the question of how one would determine what a healthy chicken liver looks like.

FLOWERS FOR WEDDINGS

Certain flowers have symbolic meanings and nobody can say for sure where these came from. The chronicler suspects that cunning florists might have something to do with it.Here follows another list:

Apple Blossom – Better things to come
Camelia – Graditude
Carnation – Fascination and love
Chrysanthemum (red) – I love you
Chrysanthemum (white) – Truth
Cyclamen – Modesty and shyness
Daffodil – Regard
Daisy – Innocence
Fern – Fascination and sincerity
Flowering Almond – Hope

Forget-me-not – True love and remembrance
Heliotrope – Devotion and faithfulness
Honeysuckle – Generosity
Hyacinth – Loveliness
Hydrangea – Boastfulness
Iris – Warmth of affection
Ivy – Eternal fidelity
Japonica – Loveliness
Jasmine – Amiability
Lemon Blossom – Fidelity in love
Lilac (white) – Youthful innocence
Lily – Majesty
Lily-of-the-valley – Return of happiness
Magnolia – Perseverance
Maidenhair – Discretion
Mimosa – Sensitivity
Orange Blossom – Purity and virginity
Peach Blossom – Captive
Rose (red) – Love
Rose (yellow) – Friendship
Rose (coral) – Desire
Rose (peach) – Modesty
Rose (dark pink) – Thankfulness
Rose (pale pink) – Grace
Rose (orange) – Fascination
Rose (white) – Innocence
Rosemary – Remembrance
Snowdrop – Hope
Sweet Pea – Delicate pleasures
Tulip – Love
Veronica – Fidelity
Violet – Faithfulness

FLOWERS ASSOCIATED WITH WEDDING ANNIVERSARIES

This list is rather arbitrary. Different books of reference will show endless variations.

1st	Pansy	12th	Peony
2nd	Lily of the Valley	13th	Chrysanthemum
3rd	Fuchsia	14th	Dahlia
4th	Hydrangea	15th	Rose
5th	Daisy	20th	Aster
6th	Calla Lily	25th	Iris
7th	Freesia	28th	Orchid
8th	Clematis	30th	Sweet pea
9th	Bird of paradise	40th	Nasturtium
10th	Daffodil	50th	Violet
11th	Tulip		

Following the 50th wedding anniversary, it's difficult to imagine a better gift than one of those Californian redwood trees that continue to thrive for up to 1,800 years: a bit difficult to transport though.

NAMES OF WEDDING ANNIVERSARIES

Common to most nations, these include:

Wooden	5th	Pearl	30th
Tin	10th	Ruby	40th
Crystal	15th	Golden	50th
China	20th	Diamond	60th
Silver	25th		

THE SEX FACTOR (and a few others)

The human female is the only mammal not to be constrained in sexual pleasure by the period of oestrus. (Oestrus means that recurrent state of sexual excitability during which the female of most mammals will accept the male.) As ovulation approaches, the human female tends to take a more provocative approach to her style of dressing. At the same time, her voice becomes higher pitched.

The London School of Economics has made a study about the best time to have sex. It reveals that 'natural cortisol levels which stimulate sex hormones are at their peak on Thursday mornings'. One supposes that adjustments have to be made for those couples not living in London.

The average life expectancy for a man in the UK is 78.1 years. The average life expectancy for a woman in the UK is 82.1 years.

If the human sperm lacks the protein known as PLCz, it can result in male infertility. This protein is essential in the process of dividing the cells to form an embryo. However, the British Fertility Society has described research in which an artificial protein can be substituted for PLCz, which greatly enhances the chance of pregnancy in those couples undergoing IVF treatment.

The average spermatozoa count of the 35-year-old French male in 1989 was 73.8 per milliliter. By 2005, this had dropped to 49.9 per milliliter (from the journal *Human Reproduction*). Presumably these statistics were not garnered from just one exhausted Frenchman.

The Sanskrit word for female genitalia is *yoni*, which means 'sacred place'.

The Sanskrit word for penis is *pasas*, meaning 'to go inside'.

At the Institute for Advanced Study of Human Sexuality in California, it is possible to read for a PhD in Sexuality.

Ivanka Savic of the Karolinska Institute in Stockholm has found that when women and gay men inhale a hormonal component in men's sweat, a brain scan shows lit-up areas around the hypothalamus area of the brain, which reflects the sexual response to the stimulus.

Luteinising hormone is a key building block of female sexual desire and is one of the triggers that ratchets up the female sex drive.

Margaret Sangar opened the first birth-control clinic in New York in 1916.

The first contraceptive pill to be approved by the FDA came on the market in 1960 (Pincus, Rock and Chang).

Martin Matzuk developed the JQI male contraceptive drug in 2012.

Before modern medical science taught us better, it was believed that the left side of a man's scrotum produced girl babies, and the right testicle produced boy babies. Due to this erroneous belief, men endured many painful constraints over the centuries in an attempt to produce offspring of the required sex.

Thirty minutes of vigorous sex burns off 200 calories; 20,160 minutes of an average lifetime is spent kissing.

In Hong Kong, until modern times, wives were allowed to kill adulterous husbands, so long as they used their bare hands.

The average length of an adult male human's penis is five inches. It is not known how many men took part in this particular survey.

The Japanese disapprove of sex toys that accurately resemble phalluses. Hence the addition of a 'smiley face' on the tips of Japanese vibrators.

Doctors originally used the vibrator in the 19th century to relieve female hysteria.

During the Second World War, the government issued the following prophylactic advice: 'Put on before you put in'.

Celery produces pheromones, which attract women.

During the years 1707–82, the wife of Feofor Vassilyev – a Russian – gave birth to 69 children, including 16 pairs of twins, 7 sets of triplets and 4 sets of quads; 67 of these children survived infancy.

During the sex act, on average, 70 per cent of men reach orgasm but only 30 per cent of women achieve it.

Guys and gals lose their virginity at about the same time, on average, with the Kinsey Institute estimating the average age of first intercourse for guys is 16.9 and gals 17.4. The Kinsey Institute (founded in 1947) is still going strong. Its research focuses on sex, gender and reproduction.

In certain parts of the United States, it is illegal to marry the spouse of a grandparent, even if one is deceased. Specifically, the States are: Maine, Maryland, South Carolina and Washington DC.

In Montana it is a felony for a wife to open her husband's mail.

Also in Montana, it is illegal for married women to go fishing alone on Sundays. Unmarried women are not permitted to fish alone at all.

In Pennsylvania ministers are prohibited from performing marriages if either the bride or the groom is drunk.

The Finns have a way to predict the number of progeny a couple will have. After the ceremony, they count the number of pieces of confetti (it used to be rice) that remain stuck in the bride's hair. It is to be wished that she does not use a particularly sticky hair spray.

Czechs haven't got round to using confetti yet. They still hurl peas. Certain developing states in Africa cover the newly-weds in a barrage of corn kernels.

There's an old folk custom for selecting a husband when there is a bewildering choice of suitors. Each eager swain's name is written on a separate onion. All the onions are stored in a cool cellar. The first onion to sprout determines which man the damsel should choose to marry. (In Shakespeare's *The Merchant of Venice*, the suitors have to guess which of three caskets is the one which will provide the key to the daughter's heart.)

A French custom, still practised in remote areas, is for the bride to step on an egg before crossing the threshold of her new home.

Years ago, in Yorkshire, when the bride made a visit to her parental home, a plate was thrown out of the window. If the plate broke, life with her new husband looked rosy. If the plate remained intact, her future was grim.

In some parts of Greece, it is a wedding tradition to write the names of all single female friends and relatives of the bride on the sole of her shoes. After the ceremony, the shoes are examined and those whose names have worn off are destined to be next in line for married bliss.

Twenty-four states in America uphold impotence as grounds for divorce.

Until recently, in Russia, any couple who lived together for two years – and could prove it – were considered to be married. It was sometimes called 'a citizen marriage'.

On 15 August 1193, Philip II of France married the Princess Ingeborg of Denmark. The next morning, Phillip changed his mind and Ingeborg fled to a convent. Despite all efforts to patch up the marriage, Phillip remained adamant. Ingeborg spent the next 20 years imprisoned in various French castles.

In ancient Britain, a green wedding dress was considered unlucky unless worn by an Irish bride. Promiscuity was attributed to a woman wearing 'a green gown', the rationale being that the greenness was as a result of rolling around on a grassy knoll with a lover.

Studies have been made that indicate sex is more frequent amongst Protestants and Jews who are married to Catholics.Apparently, other combinations of interfaith marriages do not score so well.

Photographers are not permitted at Quaker weddings, but since little is said and little is done at a Quaker wedding, there is not much to photograph anyway.

Saudi Arabian women can obtain a divorce if their husbands refuse them coffee.

In 1980, Harry Bidwell of Brighton, aged 101, divorced his wife, aged 65. One wonders what kept him.

In medieval times, a man could claim grounds for divorce should his wife be too passionate.

Until the 19th century, it is said that Egyptian men hired servants to deflower their brides for them.

Chapter 6

Traditions

CONFETTI

As with many rituals concerning birth, marriage and death, the origin of confetti is probably pagan. But it's likely that even the Romans had forgotten the reason why they threw tasteless cakes over the married couple at the end of a wedding. It had its roots in bestowing fertility rites. The centuries rolled on and so did the continual showering of sweets, raisins, nuts and rice on generations of hapless newly-weds. It has become a tradition, its genesis barely in our latent memory.

Henry VII was the last king of England to win his crown on the field of battle when, as Henry Tudor, Earl of Richmond, he defeated Richard III, the last king of the House of York, at Bosworth Field in 1485. He made a shrewd choice of wife, marrying Elizabeth of York, on 18 January 1486. By doing so, he united the two warring houses, York and Lancaster. The white and red roses were combined to form the Tudor rose. Elizabeth was daughter of Edward IV, the sister of Edward V, the niece of Richard III, and the mother of Henry VIII. Apart from that, she was Queen of England, and her profile was the model for the Queen you see in every pack of cards. Henry went to Bristol to show off his new Queen and as they paraded amongst their subjects, they were showered with wheat – the first recorded incident in Britain of confetti being thrown.

At wedding ceremonies in Italy during the 14th century, the hoity-toity threw flowers and sugared almonds over the lucky couple. The hoi polloi, not to be outdone, threw eggs and rotten fruit at the hoity-toity. Riots resulted.

In 1597, the governor of the Duchy of Milan (Juan Fernández de Velasco, 1550–1613) banned the throwing of eggs, fruit and *squittaroli* (spraying liquids) in the street. Consequently, a less volatile type of missile was chosen: confetti.

In Italian, the original word for confetti was *coriandoli.* This is because confetti consisted originally of sugar-coated coriander seeds (*coriandoli*; *confetti* is the Italian for sweets). Buying such candies wholesale proved expensive. Soon, cheaper alternatives were found and it became all the rage to hurl chalk candy balls (*benis de gess*) at each other. This sport quickly grew out of hand. Street battles developed and injuries were sustained. By the middle of the 19th century candy balls had been banned as well.

In 1875, a Milanese engineer called Enrico Mangili de Crescenzago discovered an outlet for the by-product of perforated paper used in sericulture for breeding silkworms. He decided these tiny circles of chewed paper would be perfect to scatter over the crowds at the forthcoming Milan Cranevale parade, which is organised each year soon after Shrove Tuesday. Amazingly, this paper-throwing caught the public imagination. Within 10 years, the bedding material that had been formerly the exclusive property of recumbent silkworms was now being chucked with abandon over processions everywhere, especially at weddings.

LEAP YEAR

For a calendar to remain 'in synch' with an astronomical year, it is necessary to add an extra day every four years. In those parts of the world that use the Gregorian calendar, the day chosen to be 'extra' is the last day of February. Instead of the normal 28 days, it expands to 29 in a leap year. (In the Hebrew calendar, a 13th lunar month is added into the 3rd, 6th, 8th, 11th, 14th, 17th and 19th year before the cycle starts again.)

Tradition has it that St Brigid of Kildare (the same lady who came to the City of London and founded St Bride's church) persuaded St Patrick to allow spinsters to propose on leap days. In medieval times the leap year would have fallen on 24th February – 'bissextile' day, a Latin-derived word denoting the extra day in leap year.

A corollary: legend has it that once this indulgence to the ladies had been acceded, St Brigid fell to her knees and asked St Patrick to marry her. He refused. Let us pause to consider this. St Patrick was already 66 years old when St Brigid was born in about AD 453. If she had made such a proposal even as early as her teens, Patrick would have been in his eighties. Perhaps he turned her down on the grounds that as he had been born in Cumbria he didn't want to wed a foreigner. Let's face it – most legends don't stand up to scrutiny.

This brings to mind a story regarding Angela Burdett-Coutts, of the family of Coutts Bank fame. On 7 February 1847, when she was 33, she proposed to the Duke of Wellington who was 78. He turned her down, although shortly afterwards he had a special staircase built so she could visit his bedroom. There was method behind her request. Young Angela, being one of the richest women in the world, sought solace with a man whom she could be sure was not marrying her for her money. It turned out that it was not her money the Iron Duke was after. Being a bit spartan, he slept on an old army single bed, though this did not appear to deter any late-night frivolities.

Until relatively modern times, the 29 February was

deemed not to exist. A leap day was not recognised in English law and it was 'leapt over' in legal documents. This anomaly allowed all manner of illegal things to take place on a leap day, without threat of criminal proceedings. Ladies could take advantage of this because making any sort of promise had no legal status. It became the only day of the year when a woman could propose to a man.

Ladies who were going to 'pitch woo' were expected to give notice of their intentions by wearing scarlet petticoats. Men grew wary of the whole leap year palaver, dimly suspicious that it was a feminine plot. There is yet another tradition whereby if the object of desire refuses the lady's proposal, he is obliged by way of compensation to buy her a new frock or a pair of gloves.

BUNDLING

The new *Shorter Oxford English Dictionary* gives, as one of its definitions of the verb 'to bundle': 'To sleep in one's clothes with another person, especially as a former local custom during courtship'.

There's an old rhyme, quoted mostly in Wales:

> Happy's the wooing
> That's not long adoing.

Sounds as if that ghastly poet was making another attempt to get into an anthology.

Today, the practice of bundling may be misconstrued as 'heavy petting', but until recently it was an established courtship procedure in which a couple spent the night together in bed, getting to know each other intimately through various means of mutual gratification but falling short of penetrative sex. Usually, bundling occurred in the home of the female with the tacit approval of her parents. The practice proved popular and spread like wildfire across the world until it eventually reached New England in the United States.

In the Netherlands, the custom is called '*queesten*'. The Swiss-German counterpart is '*kiltgang*', and in southern Germany the nearest equivalent descriptions are '*fenstreln*' or '*nachtfreien*', though this latter practice involves climbing in through a window.

Bundling had bonus benefits on long, cold winter evenings. It saved on fuel. An 18th-century verse declared:

> Since in a bed a man and a maid
> May bundle and be chaste,
> It is not good to burn out wood –
> It is a needless waste.

Perpetrators of bundling did not need to use the excuse of fuel economy in order to have a pre-marital cuddle. Even Puritanical souls could rely on the Bible to set a precedent. In the Book of Ruth, the eponymous heroine is portrayed in an act of virtuous binding with Boaz on the threshing floor. 'Tarry this night, and it shall be in the morning, that if he will perform unto thee the part of a kinsman, well; let him do the kinsman's part: but if he will not do the part of a kinsman to thee, then will I do the part of a kinsman to thee, as the Lord liveth: lie down until the morning' (Ruth 3:13). A couple of verses later, one learns that Ruth lay down until the morning and he rewarded her with six measures of barley, which she took to her mother-in-law, who realised immediately what had been going on. Those old wives could tell some tales.

In late 1969, in Pottstown, Pennsylvania, a group of religious-minded teenagers formed a 'Society to Bring Back Bundling'. It was not a rebellion against the Swinging Sixties but rather a nostalgic attempt to create safe and decent alternatives to sexual encounters in parked cars. Reportedly, there has been a resurgence of a desire amongst young American Christian women to retain their virginity until they marry.

Bundling had always been popular, as demonstrated by the existence of the Pennsylvanian centreboard – a wide board running through the length of the bed in which the bundlers are embracing, and theoretically preventing the frisky couple from getting close enough to risk pregnancy. In Wales, where the idea started, they used a bolster pillow as a divider.

SADIE HAWKINS DAY

In the United States, during the middle of the 20th century, there used to be a widely read syndicated comic strip called *Li'l Abner*. The eponymous anti-hero was a slow-witted hillbilly hunk. Al Capp wrote and drew the strip for 43 years from 13 August 1934.

Sadie Hawkins was a female character in the strip. She first came into prominence on 15 November 1937. Ms Hawkins was driven frantic by the lack of suitors 'comin' a courtin'', something which touched an empathetic chord in the consciousness of the nation.

Soon, in real life, a national 'Sadie Hawkins Day' came into being, held on the first Saturday each November. On this day, according to the new legend, women have the right to chase after unmarried men to propose marriage. The men line up at the gate and when the starting pistol fires, they run as if their entire future depends on it, which in some cases it does. After giving them a head start, the women tear after the men like greyhounds chasing frightened rabbits. Some men do get captured. Some just keep running.

GRETNA GREEN

Gretna Green is a village in Dumfries and Galloway (a region in south-west Scotland) and has been involved in weddings since 1754. It is one of the top destinations for marriages in the United Kingdom.

Historically it was the first staging post in Scotland on the old coaching route from London to Edinburgh. One in every six Scottish marriages takes place there. Each year it hosts more than 5,000 weddings. Its fame as a destination for 'runaway marriages' began in 1754 when the Marriage Act in England was altered so that parents who objected to the engagement of their offspring under the age of 18, could forcibly prevent the marriage from going ahead. The Parliamentary Act did not apply to Scotland, where 12 was the marriageable age for girls and 14 for boys, with or without parental consent.

The intention of the English Law Lord who introduced this Marriage Act, Lord Hardwicke, was to stop the practice of 'handfasting' ceremonies (see page 103). Stopping quickie marriages in England had the effect of multiplying them in Gretna Green.

The smithy at Gretna Hall drew the attention for runaway couples from England. The local blacksmith and his anvil became symbols for underage couples seeking marriage, for the smithy was allowed to conduct the ceremony, as long as two reliable witnesses were in attendance. The blacksmith thence became known as 'the anvil priest'. At the conclusion of the ceremony, he would place a spoonful of gunpowder on his anvil and strike it with a red-hot iron causing a minor explosion. This deafening thunderbolt alerted everyone in the village that yet another couple had become man and wife.

In 1856, the Scottish law was changed to require 21 days residency before anybody was allowed to marry. This was rescinded in 1977 and is no longer a requirement. In 1929, the law in Scotland was altered so that no couple under the age of 16 could get married, but if they were above that age no parental consent was called for. In 1940, another law was passed whereby marriages could be conducted only by an authorised registrar or a church minister. A lot of blacksmiths became registrars and a couple even took Holy Orders. Today, there are a variety of venues catering for weddings in Gretna Green, but in each case, the ceremony still takes place around an anvil.

In 1826, a famous wedding called 'the Shrigley Abduction' took place. Thirty-year-old Edward Gibbon Wakefield arrived at Gretna Green with a 15-year-old heiress, Ellen Turner. An anvil priest was found to marry them and afterwards they immediately fled to France. Consternation followed when it was discovered that this was the second time Edward Wakefield had married a rich woman. Ten years before he had eloped to Scotland with 17-year-old Eliza Pattle, whose mother accepted the arrangement and settled £70,000 on the couple. Eliza had since died. The marriage between Edward and Ellen Turner was eventually annulled by Parliament and Edward was jailed for three years.

In Jane Austen's epistolary novel, *Love and Friendship*, an impressionable juvenile girl is persuaded to elope to Gretna Green, and in *Pride and Prejudice* another couple make that particular journey (Chapter 47).

The fees for a civil marriage ceremony performed by a registrar at Anvil Hall in Gretna Green are: Monday to Friday: £245; Saturday: £325; Sunday and Bank Holidays: £366. (Note: prices are liable to change).

QUEENLY PROPOSALS

Etiquette suggests that a man should not make a proposition of marriage to a ruling monarch. Possibly, this stems from the days of Queen Elizabeth I. It is believed that the Earl of Essex proposed marriage to the Queen, and he ended up being the last person to be beheaded in the Tower of London. Subsequently, somewhat like a woman during a leap year, the Queen herself must make the request.

When Queen Victoria famously proposed to Prince Albert, he wrote afterwards:

> The queen sent for me alone to her room a few days ago, and declared to me in a genuine outburst of love and affection that I had gained her whole heart, and would make her intensely happy if I would make her the sacrifice of sharing her life with her, for she said she looked on it as a sacrifice. The only thing which troubled her was that she did not think that she was worthy of me. The joyous openness of manner in which she told me this quite enchanted me, and I was quite carried away by it. She is really most good and amiable, and I am quite sure Heaven has not given me into evil hands, and that we shall be happy together. Since that moment Victoria does whatever she fancies I should wish or like, and we talk together a great deal about our future life, which she promises me to make as happy as possible.'

Queen Victoria, a copious diarist, wrote:

> How I will strive to make him feel as little as possible the great sacrifice he has made! I told him it was a great sacrifice on his part, but he would not allow it. I then told him to fetch Ernest (Albert's brother), who congratulated us both and seemed very happy.

CARRYING THE BRIDE OVER THE THRESHOLD

At some time or other, most of us in the Western world have chuckled over cartoons depicting Flintstone-type men dragging captive females into their caves. Actually, such images may not be too far from the truth. Many modern ceremonies are symbolic and have their origins in the folk-memory of ancient times. For instance, it's been mooted that the ritual of the modern-day husband staggering under the weight of his new wife as they cross the threshold of the marital home is a throwback to that caveman dragging in his captive bride.

Around 30,000 years ago, peripatetic European modern humans lived in such places as the caves of Lascaux in southern France. It appears that the Dordogne has always been popular with tourists. There, the inhabitants whiled away the heavy hours daubing the walls with what we now call 'cave paintings'. For them, it was the latest thing in modern art. With a little imagination, one might picture our primitive ancestors, after a vigorous day's hunting, without the benefit of colour charts or paint brushes, having a bash at decorating while the little woman plucks the dinner. Thus life meandered on somewhat hand to mouth (and sometimes handprint to wall) for about 25,000 years...

But the tradition of carrying over the threshold has several possible origins (see Threshold, page 175).

HEN NIGHTS

A wedding is the perfect excuse for a girl's night out. For a number of reasons it's best to choose a night at least a week before the Big Day. The men, who invariably leave this sort of thing until the eve of the wedding, will turn up the following day pale-faced and sheepish; the bride, by contrast, will be fully recovered and look radiant. From a feminine point of view, this gives the new wife a distinct edge at the start of her journey through the occasionally rocky waters of married life.

To celebrate the countdown to the end of her singleton existence, her friends in the sisterhood will invariably throw a farewell party for the bride to be. In more austere days, this took place in somebody's bedsit where old pals met up and sat around a bottle of cooking sherry wallowing in nostalgia. In the 21st century, it is more likely to be in a hired hall or restaurant. The venue is festooned with pink balloons, often with a 'Learner' (L) symbol printed on them. The focus of the evening might even be a strip show consisting of well-preserved young men with healthy six-packs (Viking helmets optional). The entertainment lasts up to two and a half hours. There are three distinct types of show available:

1. 'The full monty': a show that goes 'all the way', right down to willy-waving, which does not always suit the susceptibilities of older guests although grannies tend to bow out of hen nights. If they do go along, who knows, it may turn out to be a nostalgic experience.

2. A 'no-show show': in this type of show the hunks strip down to their thongs but keep their bits and bobs hidden. Again, this might not be to everybody's taste. Some of the more raucous guests might well demand a little more.

3. 'A body building display': frustrating but nice, this show is old fashioned but titillating – best imagined as well-greased bodies in 'Me Tarzan – You Jane' poses. When this option is selected, the evening may be topped off with a drag queen. His jewelled stilettos will catch any girl's heart, and many women have a certain empathy with camp humour.

In London's West End there is a club called Madame Jojo's – a cabaret club, dark and enticing – that has become a favaoured venue for hen-night parties, its Kitsch Cabaret being particularly popular.

BRIDES OF CHRIST

In the Catholic Church there are more than 3,000 consecrated virgins worldwide. These are women (not nuns) who give themselves totally to Christ. Their mission stems from the words of Jesus as quoted by Matthew (19), in which he acknowledges that some will not marry, for the sake of the kingdom of heaven. They also stand as witnesses to future resurrection when, according to Mark (12:25), Jesus said: 'When they rise from the dead they neither marry nor are given in marriage.'

Judith Stegman, president of the United States Association of Consecrated Virgins, said the strict requirements ensure that there are few women who are able to become brides of Christ: 'We're talking about someone who has never knowingly and willingly given herself in sexual union with a man.... We're giving our virginity, that which we've always kept intact, to Christ.'

Miss Stegman explained why nuns would not necessarily qualify: 'The woman who's making a vow of chastity to a religious order could have been married before. The consecrated virgin doesn't need that vow.' In short, a nun need not be a virgin, whereas virginity is the prerequisite to becoming a Bride of Christ.

Consecrated virgins continue with their everyday working lives and do not go to convents. 'We live in total imitation of the Blessed Virgin Mary. She lived her life entirely in the world... Sometimes we'll smile and say she's our mother-in-law,' Miss Stegman added. The vocation was banned for centuries until reinstated by Pope John Paul II (Pontiff 1978– 2005).

MARRIAGE IN THE EARLY CHRISTIAN ERA

Early Christian thinkers such as Augustine (AD 354–430) and Jerome (AD 347–420) were deeply perturbed by the sexual act. From their readings of St Paul to the Corinthians they extrapolated only one redeeming factor for sex: marriage. And to their stoic way of thinking, marriage itself had only one purpose: procreation. It followed that the relationship between a man and woman prior to getting married must remain chaste. Virginity became the new ideal.

However, this concept wasn't half as much fun as people had been having under the Romans, and it took a lot of church law and threats of eternal damnation to get the message across. Jerome took his newfound authority to extremes. He preached that as well as abstaining from sex, men should live in poverty – preferably with other men in monastic penance. The Middle Ages were tough. Food, shelter and warmth were all at a premium. Monasteries provided these essentials in return for the abnegation of sin, sex and ambition.

Marriage was an escape, but the conditions required to achieve matrimony were grim. The difficulty was compounded by a reconciliation of the notion of marriage as a sacrament, with the edict that sex was a base and evil act.

Women showed signs of frustration. In an attempt to find out what they could do to make themselves more attractive to men, they sometimes went to extremes. During the Renaissance it became fashionable for women to pluck their hairline to give themselves higher foreheads. For weddings, their hair would be washed and allowed to hang loose, with flowers woven in to form a floral crown; at the time this was quite a daring thing to do.

It took a thousand years of torturous evolution for Christian marriage customs to emerge in the form we recognise today, wherein mutual consent to a marriage must be given freely without family coercion, and where the agreed purpose of the partnership is not necessarily procreation.

In general, during the Middle Ages love was not the reason for marriage. The aim of the upper class was the acquisition of wealth and power. Ceremonies took place in the courtyards or Great Hall of their castles. Among the lower classes, where poverty was rife, however, weddings often took place as the result of pregnancy. Many marriages were mere business arrangements. Couples were generally too poor to even exchange rings. Instead, sometimes a coin was broken in half, the bride taking one half and the groom the other. These were the original 'love tokens'.

Wedding gifts were perfunctory and utilitarian. The most a bride could look forward to were wooden utensils for cooking and washing. If they obeyed the Ten Commandments they wouldn't get locked up. Uneducated as most peasants were, a wife would expect nothing more than the agony of childbirth – probably at least once a year – together with a life of drudgery. It was small wonder that the church with its offer of a pain-free afterlife held everyone in its thrall.

Under canon – that is, ecclesiastical – law, the minimum age for marriage was 14 for boys and 12 for girls. Being sexual animals, men and women did not automatically conform to the Christian credo. Couples carried on cohabiting, and some committed bigamy. Secular law did not necessarily correspond with canon law and the church found it increasingly difficult to keep people's sex lives under its authority.

In 1215, the Fourth Lateran Council produced a new law insisting that banns had to be published before the ceremony, and that marriages must be conducted in public under the auspices of an ordained priest.

Another 350 years rolled by, and along came Protestant reformers, Martin Luther (1483–1546) and John Calvin (1509–64). They argued that sex was not evil but a natural act, a God-given attribute to be enjoyed and that it was perfectly permissible to fire blanks until ready. This enlightened thinking made marriage popular again. People started to marry for the simple reason that they fancied each other. So long as the church just officiated and kept the record straight, marriage became something to look forward to.

Hundreds of years later, in the second half of the 20th century, two issues cropped up that threatened to rock the boat: 1) birth control and 2) marital sexuality. Procreation was no longer the prime reason for marriage. Marital affection took preference, and the church did not like it. The state made civil marriages readily accessible, and the church discovered it was gradually losing its flock.

In the 21st century, the acceptability of same-sex marriages has continued to loosen the screw on canon law.

DROIT DE SEIGNEUR

This term is also known as *jus primae noctis* ('right of the first night'). Legend has it that lords of the manor and heads of clans in medieval Europe had the feudal right to take the maidenhead from a bride on the wedding night if she married one if his vassals. This is a dubious claim and seems to stem from books written in the 15th century by disaffected French noblemen who, one suspects, were guilty of wishful thinking.

Another school of thought is that the threat of such a deed was held over the vassals' heads like a Damocles's sword, which they could only avert by paying their overlord extra dues in lieu.

THE BLOOD-RED WEDDING

The 18-year-old Marguerite de Valois, sister of King Charles IX of France, was forced to marry Henry, the King of Navarre, in a marriage designed to reignite friendly relations between the Catholics and the Huguenots. In reality, the marriage had been arranged by Catherine de' Medici, the bride's mother, in order to assassinate the Protestants when they arrived in Paris for the wedding, which took place on

18 August 1572. At the end of the celebrations on 24 August, which happened to be Saint Bartholomew's Day, the massacre began. When it was over, it is estimated 30,000 people had been killed – hence 'the blood-red wedding', as the nuptials came to be called.

Chapter 7

How it all Began

THE CONCEPT OF MARRIAGE

For thousands of years, our hunter-gatherer ancestors wandered from place to place searching for food before they discovered the benefits of settling down. Gradually, they developed agriculture and invented farms.

An estate develops in the owner a feeling of permanence. As land represented something material that one day would have to be handed on to the kids, heirs became not just desirable but positively necessary. The early farmers encouraged their sons and daughters to hunker down and do some serious mating. Neighbouring farmers would trade in their daughters to get a piece of the action. As a bonus, these 'marriage contracts' lessened the chances of feuding between adjacent landowners.

Old habits died slowly. Wives were for procreation; concubines were for pleasure. As the marriage concept evolved, the 'harem habit' didn't disappear overnight. Tribal dynasties became established. Later, as religious beliefs took hold, the concepts of romantic love and chivalry were added to the mix. Matrimony came into existence.

The word 'matrimony' comes from the Latin, *matrimonium*, the implication being that the wife is heading for a state of motherhood (*mater*). In Greco-Roman culture, the production of legitimate children was the prime purpose of marriage. It was strictly a monogamous affair. (With the exception of the Spartans – and it's just as well our forefathers didn't follow their example. See page 224.)

Early Christianity mimicked the marriage laws of the Romans by adopting some of their – to Christians – pagan ways, but the ultimate purpose of marriage was, above all, to produce children, to protect property and to promote good citizenship. This was the case in ancient Greece too. A father would give away his daughter with the words: 'I pledge my daughter for the purpose of producing legitimate offspring.' If no children were produced, the disappointed husband could give the daughter back to her father.

The Roman *confarreatio* was a type of upper-class marriage in Rome. The happy couple ate cakes, the ingredients of which included spelt flour (*farreus*) and salt. Such privileges, dubious as they may seem to us, were reserved for those born into the ruling class. As the centuries rolled by, high-spirited Roman wags, instead of chewing them, started throwing these cakes at the couples. They probably tasted awful anyway. Over the centuries, as salt-and-flour cakes lost their piquancy, alternative symbols of fertility began to be thrown at the lucky couple: nuts, rice, confectionary, dried fruit…

And confetti was born (see page 120).

WHO CAME UP WITH THE IDEA?

The word 'wed' means 'a pledge' in Old English. The pledge comes in the form of a ring that a man gives a woman: it represents his bond that he will honour the contract. The symbolism lies in the shape of it. A ring, being circular, has no end, therefore their bond will be eternal – our forefathers were nothing if not optimistic.

'With this ring I do thee wed.' But without end? How did this come about?

Before civilisation had taken root, a man would capture his woman from another tribe and, with the help of his 'best man', keep her hidden in a secret place where her family could not find her. The honeymonth (or, as we say now, honeymoon) was the length of time it took for her tribe to catch up with her. After a month or so, she would, with luck, be pregnant, and in that event, her own family gave up on her.

When agriculture evolved and 'land' became something to possess, the woman chosen to be a wife would be bartered like a mere object in exchange for land or animals. She would then be owned by the husband, and be part of his 'goods and chattels'. The word 'chattels' refers to any item of movable personal property, such as furniture, domestic animals – or a wife.

If we could step back in time, the earliest age that we might find the wedding ceremony recognisable as the prototype of what we know today in this country would be shortly after the Battle of Hastings. In 1076 the Council of Westminster decreed that 'no man should give his daughter or female relative to anyone without priestly blessing'. Later councils decreed that all marriages must be open to the public and not be held in secret (see Appendix 2). In 1215, marriage was declared one of the church's seven sacraments, alongside rites such as baptism and penance.

Medieval rules forbidding marriage during penitential seasons, on high festival days and after mid-day are long gone. Civil marriages became legal in 1836, and it became possible for non-conformists and Catholics to be married in their own places of worship.

Until Lord Hardwicke promoted the Marriage Act in 1753, marriages could take place anywhere so long as they were conducted before an ordained clergyman of the Church of England. This enabled wealthy couples to marry while at least one of the partners was under age, under licence. The Marriage Act ensured that marriages took place in a church or chapel of the Church of England. Nobody under the age of 21 could get married without parental consent. Clergymen who flouted this law were liable to receive 14 years' transportation.

Since 1929, the minimum age to marry, for either sex, is 16.

MARRIED WOMEN'S PROPERTY RIGHTS

With the colonisation of America in the late 15th century came the importation of European laws. As in English law, as soon as a man and woman married, they became one person and the wife's role was defined as 'feme covert', which meant she was subordinate to her husband. The process of female emancipation began in 1771 with the Act to Confirm Certain Conveyances and Directing the Manner of Proving Deeds to be Recorded. Effectively, this meant that a married man could not sell goods accumulated in a marriage without the approval of his wife. In 1809, a law was passed in Connecticut allowing women to create and execute wills. New York caught up 39 years later, championed by Elizabeth Stanton, Paulina Davis and Ernestine Rose. In terms of female property rights, it was hailed as one of the most significant improvements of all time to the cause.

The granddaughter of the playwright Richard Brinsley Sheridan was instrumental in changing the laws on behalf of women in England. Caroline Norton (1808–77) was married to George Norton, a profligate MP who lost his money and gave her nothing. She started writing and began to earn good money. George took advantage of the laws of the time and confiscated all his wife's income, claiming that everything she had belonged to him. Barely able to feed her children,

Caroline got her own back by running up enormous bills in her husband's name, claiming that all her debts were his.

Not taking this lightly, George accused her of conducting an affair with the Prime Minister (Lord Melbourne), which was vehemently denied and thrown out of court, nearly overthrowing Parliament in the process. Even so, George would not divorce Caroline and took possession of their three sons because at that time the law insisted children were the legal property of the father. Caroline campaigned to change the law and eventually managed to institute the Custody of Infants Act 1839 whereby a mother could petition the courts for custody of children up to the age of seven, and for access to older children. She then went on to change the divorce laws. In one key speech she said:

> An English wife may not leave her husband's house. Not only can he sue her for restitution of 'conjugal rights,' but he has a right to enter the house of any friend or relation with whom she may take refuge…and carry her away by force…
>
> If her husband take proceedings for a divorce, she is not, in the first instance, allowed to defend herself… She is not represented by attorney, nor permitted to be considered a party to the suit between him and her supposed lover, for 'damages'.
>
> If an English wife be guilty of infidelity, her husband can divorce her so as to marry again; but she cannot divorce the husband, a vinculo, however profligate he may be…
>
> Those dear children, the loss of whose pattering steps and sweet occasional voices made the silence of [my] new home intolerable as the anguish of death…what I

> suffered respecting those children, God knows...under the evil law which suffered any man, for vengeance or for interest, to take baby children from the mother.

Her intense campaigning eventually resulted in the Married Women's Property Act 1870. The courts were forced to recognise a husband and a wife as two separate legal entities, in the same manner as if the wife was a 'feme sole' – that is, an unmarried, divorced or widowed woman with the right to own property and make contracts in her own name.

In England and Wales the Married Women's Property Act of 1882 gave women proprietorial rights on an equal footing with her male counterparts, and improvements have been added from time to time ever since.

Incidentally, men are no longer permitted to beat their wives. In the days when this was considered to be the norm, the husbands were allowed to use a stick 'no thicker than the thumb', hence the phrase, 'by rule of thumb'.

MARRIAGES IN ANCIENT ROME

The Latin expression *aquae et ignis communiciatio* was fundamental to marriage. It stood for the sharing of water and fire. In other words, the married couple agreed to share natural resources (see A Roman Wedding, below).

The concept of marriage for the Romans evolved from the mythical abduction of the Sabine women. The Roman historians Livy and Plutarch both touch on the subject of the Rape of the Sabine women, which is supposed to have occurred shortly after the foundation of Rome, around 750 BC. The myth tells us that Romulus and his followers abducted the Sabine women promising them citizenship of Rome.

The Latin word *raptio*, which translates as 'rape', had the connotation of 'abduction' in the past. Livy makes the point that no sexual assault took place; that the women were offered 'honourable wedlock and civil rights, and – the greatest honour of all in nature – they would be the mothers of Free men.'

In the earliest days of the Empire, a woman's possessions automatically passed into the hands of the husband as soon as she married him; she was subjugated to him. It was only towards the end of the decline of the Roman Empire that her property remained separate.

Soldiers serving in the Roman Army, under the rank of Centurion, were not permitted to marry. This rule was relaxed by the second century AD, and a Roman citizen could marry after his period of military service. This accounted for the fact that most men eligible for marriage were in their mid-20s, whereas women were typically aged between 15 and 20.

There were other obstacles. Restrictions were imposed upon actors, prostitutes and women over the age of 50 as to whom they could marry.

For the noble Roman, the concept of citizenship – what we might call today 'national identity' – was paramount. Good citizenship was the entire reason for being Roman. If a Roman citizen married a foreigner, then the marriage was not recognised. Nor could a Roman woman marry a slave. It followed that most marriages were arranged.

In the third century AD the Roman lawmaker Modestinus formulated the classical definition of marriage: 'Marriage is the joining of a man and a woman and their union for life by divine and human law.' Marriage in Greco-Roman times was a strictly monogamous institution, distinguishing it from other political systems of those times. Christianity followed suit.

Patria potestas, roughly translated, means 'father is in charge'. This applied to fathers of legitimate offspring, who had to obtain their fathers' consent in order to marry. Fundamentally, there were three types of marriage recognised in ancient Rome.

1. *Usus*: A marriage, which resulted from a couple cohabiting together for at least a year and a day.

2. *Coemptio*: Resulting from a more formal cohabitation where the husband had purchased the bride in some way – sometimes by payment of a symbolic token.

3. *Confarreatio*: The top-flight, official form of marriage which was required by the Roman priesthood in republican times, in which a wife becomes absorbed by her husband's family and is subject to his control (*manus*).

There were certain rituals to be observed to conclude the *confarreatio* type of union successfully. Once a couple had obtained their respective fathers' consent to a wedding proposal, a betrothal would be announced and a banquet given between the two families. The fiancé would give his pledge in the form of a ring – usually gold – to the bride-to-be. The girl's father would pay the negotiated dowry to the prospective groom. The contract would be sealed with a kiss. By the day of the wedding, all that was left was the dressing-up. On the night before the 'big day', the bride had to formally renounce all childish things and so she offered up her toys and old clothes to the gods.

The wedding itself had no legal substance. It existed to prove to the world that the young couple meant to live together – *affectio maritalis* – implying something deeper than we imagine from its modern day translation: 'marital affection'.

Choosing the right date for the wedding was complicated by a number of factors. Hollow months (those of 29 days) were unlucky; full months (those of 30 days) were therefore auspicious. The ancient Greek calendar was the template used by the Romans until the Julian calendar was introduced. The months were named in conjunction with lunar phases. The kalends, the nones and the ides of each month, and the succeeding days of each of these, were considered unlucky. Kalends (from which the word calendar is derived), originally meant the first day of the month, but that would have depended on the lunar cycle.

It is easy to see why astrologers and soothsayers were needed to sort it out. In short, February and May were the months when marriages were to be avoided. The most auspicious time was in June.

A Roman wedding

On the morning of the wedding, the bride was dressed by her mother in a white hemless tunic woven in one piece and falling to the ankles (*tunica recta*) secured at the waist by a girdle tied in a Herculean knot – nodus *Herculanus* (see True lovers' knot, page 102). The playwright Plautus poked fun at all this in his sexy farce, *Amphitryon*, written a couple of hundred years BC.

The bride's shoulders were covered in a saffron-dyed shawl (*palla*), and her hair was carefully plaited in the manner of her ancestors: six strands parted using a bent iron spearhead. Her veil and her shoes were orange.

At the house of the bride's father, there had to be at least

10 witnesses to justify the wedding. Consent had to be publicly witnessed to make the marriage official. The couple stood before a priest and the bride gave her consent thus: '*Ubi tu Gaius, ego Gaia.*' ('When-and-where you are, Gaius, I then-and-there am Gaia'). Invoking the name Gaius was supposed to bring luck to the couple.

The groom would then place the ring on his bride's finger – the one with the nerve to her heart. (To begin with, wedding rings were worn predominantly by wives. Husbands started to wear them a mere hundred or so years ago.) The bride joined a procession heading for her new home led by a youth holding aloft a torch which had been lit from a hearth in her own home. Another lad held her right hand, a third her left hand. The bridesmaids followed. Water was brought out to her from her husband's home. This was symbolic of the aforementioned *aquae et ignis communiciatio.*

Before entering the house, the torch was tossed into the air. Whoever caught it would have good luck. Today, the torch has become the wedding bouquet. Small, sweet cakes were crumbled and thrown over the bride. The Roman poet, Lucretius, describes this in the fifth book of his Epicurean poem, *De Rerum Natura*, written in the first century BC.

Roman culture was thick with omens. For example, if a bride were to trip up as she started her new life, it would be disastrous. Accordingly, the groom lifted her over the threshold.

A married woman found herself in a privileged position, respected and listened to. There was even a special day for her held at the beginning of March called The Roman Matronalia – what we might call Mother's Day.

For the first 500 years of the Roman Empire, divorce was unknown.

ROMAN MARRIAGE LAWS

Later, to split up, the Roman man and wife needed to assemble seven witnesses in front of whom the unhappy couple made clear their intention to go their separate ways. As in modern times, there could be repercussions, such as who was going to look after the children and how much of the dowry would be returned.

At the height of the Roman Empire, the legitimate birthrate of the free Roman elite began to slide due to marriage being taken less than seriously, and the higher echelon living louche and extravagant lives. It all went to prove the old cliché, 'power corrupts and absolute power corrupts absolutely'. In many cases, amongst the hierarchy, husbands and wives had started to lose respect for each other, together with the underlying purpose of marriage, that is to say – procreation.

Men enjoyed the company of slave girls, prostitutes and concubines. And women were equally adulterous. The Emperor Augustus's own daughter was so promiscuous she was exiled. As a consequence, the Roman Emperor Augustus introduced the Julian Laws (*leges Iuliae*) in 18 BC.

A speech in the Senate reflects his views: 'If we could survive without a wife, citizens of Rome, all of us would do without that nuisance; but since nature has so decreed that we cannot manage comfortably with them, nor live in any way without them, we must plan for our lasting preservation rather than for our temporary pleasure.'

In the overpopulated world of today, it is an alien concept for us to understand the principle behind the Julian Laws, which was to keep up the birthrate of the Roman citizens through a panoply of rules and penalties. The crux of the new laws was the *lex Iulia de adulteris*, which made adultery a criminal offence. A father could kill his daughter found in flagrante, along with her lover. A cuckolded husband could not kill his wife, but by law, he had to divorce her forthwith. If a man failed to divorce an adulterous wife, he could be charged with pimping for her.

Widows between 20 and 50 had to remarry within a year. Divorcees under 50 who were not in disgrace had to marry within six months. Forfeitures and tax penalties were imposed on men between 25 and 60 and women between 20 and 50 who remained unmarried or childless. All married couples were given tax incentives to have at least three freeborn children.

With the coming of Christendom the Julian laws fell into disuse.

BRIDE ABDUCTION (BRIDE KIDNAPPING)

Marriage had its origins in primitive bride abduction. In most countries kidnapping women is no longer legal, but it still goes on. Bride abduction was not deemed unusual or particularly distasteful in parts of the Old Testament (see Appendix 3).

LORD HARDWICKE

The 1st Earl of Hardwicke was an 18th-century English Lord Chancellor. He was an expert on Roman civil law, which helped him establish the principles and limits of the English system of equity. At the age of 63, he introduced his Marriage Act of 1753. The first statutory legislation in England and Wales to require a formal ceremony of marriage, it came into force on 25 March 1754.

Up until this time in Europe, common-law marriages were frequent in the Middle Ages, but their legality was abolished in Roman Catholic countries by the Council of Trent (1545–63, see Appendix 1). Common-law marriages in England were rendered invalid by Lord Hardwicke's Act.

SAME-SEX MARRIAGES

According to the ecclesiastical laws of the Church of England, known as canon law, marriage is defined as being between a man and a woman, since regeneration is the ultimate aim of the exercise. Changing the definition to introduce same-sex unions would have to be approved by the General Synod, the Church's governing body.

Notwithstanding, on 17 July 2013, the Marriage (Same Sex Couples) Act 2013 received Royal Assent. The Act will almost certainly become enshrined in Law by July 2014. However, the Church of England, the Church in Wales, and the Muslim Council of Britain have denounced this Bill. The Prime Minister David Cameron quotes, and endorses, the argument put forward by Lord Alderdice in 2004:

> One of the most fundamental rights of all is the right to have close, confiding, lasting, intimate relationships. Without them, no place, no money, no property, no ambition – nothing – amounts to any value. It seems to me a fundamental human right to be able to choose the person with whom you wish to spend your life and with whom you wish to have a real bond.

In order to illustrate the controversy leading up to the legalisation of same-sex marriages in the UK, here are extracts from two letters published on 3 June 2013 in *The Times*.

> '...Parliament has intervened to redefine the scope of marriage over the past three centuries. A majority of the public now supports same-sex marriage, and legislatures around the world are reflecting this change of attitude. The elected House of Commons passed this Bill on a free vote by more than two to one cross-party majority. The House of Lords should consider this legislation carefully, but it would be wrong to hinder a measure whose time has come.'

The signatories to this extract followed: Lord Fowler, Lord Jenkin of Roding, Lord Hunt of Wirral, Lord Deben, Baroness Bottomley of Nettlestone and Lord Garel-Jones.

And from the second letter:

> '...that this Bill has been pushed through, especially with such contempt for freedom of conscience and religion, is alien to long-held Conservative values and democratic principles...
>
> '...this Bill is politically toxic for the Conservative Party. Not only has it alienated the grassroots activists from the leadership, but it is driving our traditional voters elsewhere while failing to draw in many new ones.'

The signatories to this letter were Robert Woollard, chairman, Conservative Grassroots; and other members or former chairmen of local Conservative Associations.

The controversy is not confined to the British Isles. In June 2013, the Duma (the lower house of the Russian parliament) passed a law banning 'gay propaganda' to people under the age of 18. The Bill was passed by 436 votes to nil. Spokesperson for the Duma, Yelena Mizulina, said:

'Traditional sexual relations are between a man and a woman. It is precisely these relations that need the State's protection.' President Vladimir Putin said that the anti-propaganda law was meant to protect youth, not to impose sanctions on gays.

In Haiti there is a gay and lesbian community that has hitherto had to duck under the radar. The Haitian Coalition of Religious and Moral Organisations – a religious group – is vehemently opposed to the call for the legalization of gay marriage.

Other countries take what some consider to be an enlightened approach. In 2013, the French government sanctioned same-sex marriage, bringing the country into line with New Zealand, the Netherlands, Belgium, Spain, Canada, South Africa, Norway, Sweden, Portugal, Iceland, Argentina and Denmark. At the time of writing, Uruguay is thought to be giving serious consideration to adopting similar measures.

So far (in mid-2013), 13 US States recognise same-sex marriage: California, Connecticut, Delaware, Iowa, Maine, Massachusetts, Maryland, Minnesota, New Hampshire, New York, Rhode Island, Vermont and Washington, plus five tribal jurisdictions. The District of Columbia has already legalised same-sex marriage. It is anticipated that other States will follow and there are referenda being recommended for Colorado, Hawaii, Illinois, New Jersey, Nevada, Oregon and Wisconsin. The US Supreme Court has nullified the 'same-sex sodomy' laws in several states including Texas, Kansas, Oklahoma and Missouri.

Gay marriage, though rare, has been known through the ages. Same-sex unions were talked about in ancient Greco-Roman times (and in some regions of China, such as Fujian province). These sanctified homosexual marriages continued until the Emperor Constantine declared Christianity to be the religion of the Roman Empire.

Same-sex unions were also known in medieval Europe. There were liturgies for same-sex marriages (known as 'spiritual brotherhoods') in the 12th and 13th centuries. However, in 1306, the Byzantine Emperor Andronicus II condemned these marriages, together with sorcery and incest, as 'unchristian'.

Fifteen hundred years before the invention of the violin, Nero (AD 37–68), known to schoolchildren as the fellow who fiddled while Rome burned, became Emperor at the age of 17. Always a strange man, he became even weirder towards the end of his short life. He is alleged to have had formal marriages with at least two men. His infatuation with his first 'husband' Sporus was such that Nero had him castrated and, as far as it was possible in AD 67 had him surgically altered into a woman. Nero called him Poppaea Sabina after a deceased wife of whom he had been quite fond (although some accounts say that he killed her in a fit of rage). The wedding was conducted in public with the Senate present and all due ceremony. On their bridal conveyance during the subsequent procession, Nero and Sporus continually embraced and fondled each other to prove their love to the world. Presumably this took Nero's mind off his mother with whom he'd had an incestuous liaison before assassinating her.

His next marriage was to a freedman called Doryphorus. Willing to try anything once, this time Nero played the female role. Later, Nero could be heard screaming in the nuptial chamber, apparently in imitation of a girl being deflowered.

The patience of the Senate snapped – Nero was

proclaimed Public Enemy Number One. He botched a suicide attempt and persuaded his friends to kill themselves while he watched to show him how it was done. Following Nero's suicide, his main rival to the succession promptly sent for Nero's old buddy, the 'Empress Sporus', whom he married on the spot in an attempt to bolster his claims to be the next emperor.

A little more than a hundred years later, on 11 March, AD 222, the Praetorian Guard assassinated another man who preferred the distaff to the sceptre, the Emperor Elagabalus, at the tender age of 18. He reigned for less than four years and in that time he'd married and divorced five women and two men. His first husband was his chariot driver, Hierocles. His next marriage was to a man called Comazon. He was such a disgrace to the Roman Empire that upon his death the practice of *damnatio memoriae* was put into effect, meaning his name was systematically erased from the public record.

A law in the Theodosian Code was issued in AD 342 by the Christian emperors Constantius II and Constans, which prohibited same-sex marriage and decreed that any who contravened this edict should be executed.

Some 1,300 years later, in 1967, the Sexual Offences Act was passed in the UK. This decriminalised private homosexual acts between men aged over 21, while at the same time imposing heavier penalties on street offences.

In the Papal encyclical '*Humanae Vitae*' (Of Human Life') written in 1968, Pope Paul VI made it clear that sex and marriage 'must of necessity retain its intrinsic relationship to the procreation of life'. He continued: 'Neither is it valid to argue, as a justification for sexual intercourse which is deliberately contraceptive, that a lesser evil is to be preferred to a greater one, or that such intercourse would merge with procreative acts of past and future to form a single entity, and so be qualified by exactly the same moral goodness as these.'

The law was not changed in Scotland until 1980, and for Northern Ireland in 1982.

In 1994 the Criminal Justice and Public Order Act lowered the age of consent for gay men from 21 to 18, and in 2001 it was further lowered to 16.

To sum up, in 2013 in response to the question: 'What is the Catholic church's stance on homosexuality?' Pope Francis replied: 'Who am I to judge?' None the less, the arguments for and against same-sex marriage continue to rage in some quarters.

CONCUBINAGE

In countries where the caste system still has relevance (as among Hindus and Hasidic Jews, for example) differing social or religious status of the partners may rule out marriage. The reason that some women remain without a partner is because they receive alimony on condition that they do not remarry. There are a number of circumstances in which a woman may choose to live with a man in a matrimonially oriented state and, in effect, become his concubine.

In ancient China concubinage was legally recognised as akin to marriage, albeit at an inferior level; the offspring of these relationships were legitimately recognised. Indeed, if a man's legal wife was unable to conceive, it was not unusual for him to produce an heir by impregnating his concubine.

In ancient Rome, concubinage was an honourable de facto situation. In fact, on Roman gravestones, it was something of an honour for a woman to be described as a '*concubina*'.

A '*concubinus*' was a young male slave kept by his Roman master as a sexual plaything. This was not considered homosexual but an additional amusement to married life.

Biblically, what distinguished a wife from a concubine was that a wife had a dowry whereas a concubine did not.

POLYGAMY

Polygamy is bigamy, but on a bigger scale. It is the custom whereby one man has several wives at the same time. The female version, where a woman can have multiple bites at the cherry, living with several husbands at one time, is called polyandry.

Polygamy is tolerated in nearly 50 countries particularly in the Sahara and in Muslim communities. In Senegal, nearly 47 per cent of all marriages are multiple.

There are independent cases in the Western world where a man has lived openly with several women at the same time and declared them his wives. Certain religious extremists do not view this as polygamy and justify such conduct by citing (and misinterpreting) Messianic Judaism.

MORMONS

The founders of the Mormon movement were susceptible to spiritual revelations, particularly those brought by visitations of angels. In 1823, a man called Joseph Smith claimed to have been visited by a Christian angel called Moroni, who revealed to him an ancient Hebrew text that had been lost for 1,500 years. Over the next few years, Joe translated this work into English. In 1830, *The Book of Mormon* was published. The Church of Jesus Christ of Latter-day Saints (to give the Mormon church its formal name) was established and the practice of plural marriage was given priority.

Mormons believed that it was God's command to have several wives, quoting from the Bible (2 Samuel 12:8), in which, at the formation of the Hebrew nation, the patriarchs, Abraham and Jacob, and Kings David and Solomon, among others, all had plural marriages. ('And Nathan said to David … And I gave thee thy master's house, and thy master's wives into thy bosom, and gave thee the house of Israel and of Judah…' and so on). Joe Smith justified himself by claiming that the Angel Moroni had raised a sword and threatened to execute him if he refused to spread the word of God.

It's interesting to pause a moment and question why Joseph Smith was the chosen vehicle. Where had he come from? Joe's mother was an occultist and his father was obsessed with finding Captain Kid's hidden pirate treasure. One can only assume that at that time people weren't as cynical as we are.

According to the Doctrine and Covenants of Joseph Smith (D & C 132:63), the reason for polygamy was to multiply and replenish the earth. We might be forgiven today if we leaned towards the possibility that Joe introduced plural marriage in order to expand his own sexual opportunities. He certainly succeeded in that ambition, causing outrage amongst a number of cuckolded husbands.

On 27 June 1844, Joe and his brother were murdered in jail by a mob in Carthage, Illinois. Joe left behind 34 wives.

The Mormon church survived.

In July 1847, Smith's successor Brigham Young led the 148 remaining Mormons into the Valley of the Great Salt Lake. Brigham spent some of his time practising and encouraging polygamy, but mostly he was dodging the lawmen. When he died in 1877, he was responsible for having bereaved 17 wives and 57 children.

Three types of marriage were contracted:

a) 'Time only Matrimony' – for the term of this life only.
b) 'Eternity only' – only to last until the next life after death, thus permitting the woman to be married to a different man on earth.
c) 'Time and eternity sealings' – marriage not only for this life but for the next life, after death and forever after.

In 1890, Wilford Woodruff, president of Church of Jesus Christ of Latter-day Saints, issued a declaration which ended the practice of plural marriage. Today, it is not possible to be a polygamist and remain a member of the church. The centre of Mormon influence is in Utah, but the majority of Mormons live outside the United States.

All sexual activity outside of marriage, either hetero or homo, is considered a serious sin. Mormons who declare themselves gay or lesbian or bisexual may remain members of the Mormon church. Needless to say, there is a proviso: they must obey the law of chastity. The Mormon church has over 2,000 branches, 180 missions and more than 5 million members.

THE FUNDAMENTALIST CHURCH OF JESUS CHRIST OF LATTER-DAY SAINTS

Warren Jeffs, supported by his brother Lyle, is the living Prophet of the Fundamentalist Church of Jesus Christ of Latter-day Saints, a breakaway sect of the above, with at least 10,000 followers. Warren is currently serving a life sentence in Texas for abusing an underage 15-year-old 'bride' and fathering her child.

Discipline in this sect is rigid. The wives are not allowed mobile phones, hair ribbons, toys or brooches. It is forbidden for a female to take paid employment. Quite how Warren keeps his flock together from a prison cell, which he is expected to inhabit until he is 93, is a mystery. Perhaps there's an Angel out there helping him.

CHINESE POLYGAMY

The Chinese use a euphemism for polygamy: it is the word *ernai*, meaning mistress or 'second wife'. The penchant for second wives in the new market-oriented economy of China is fast becoming the norm. The minister of railways for China, Liu Zhijun, was removed from office in 2011 having been accused of embezzling nearly £200 million. Putting him in jail removed him from the tender mercies of at least 18 mistresses.

POLYANDRY

Polyandry is a relationship in which one woman has two or more husbands at the same time.

POLYGENY

Polygeny is the (hypothetical) origination of humankind from several independent sets of ancestors; the theory of such origination.

JEWISH AND ISLAMIC RITUALS

In antiquity, before they gained a precarious foothold in the hills of Judea, Jews were Bedouin nomads. Being a wandering race, they rejected the anthropomorphic gods of the settled peoples and created a Mosaic Law suited to their own austerity, which demanded a strict discipline imposed by the one God – Jehovah/Allah – and belief in his jealous wrath. The code laid down when King David ruled from Jerusalem has been the blueprint for matrimony to this day.

The Holy Quran permits a Muslim man to marry more than one woman at a time (up to a maximum of four), but it does not encourage this behaviour. Fifteen hundred years ago, when Sharia law was evolving, there was good reason why nomadic tribes should have more than one wife. So many women died in childbirth in the harsh conditions of the deserts that having two or three attempts at producing progeny were essential for survival.

In the 21st century, in countries governed by Sharia law, the second marriage is permitted only under special circumstances, such as an illness or the proof of infertility. Even then, the first wife's consent must be obtained. Polygamy is permitted under certain circumstances, for example, when the death of a husband has left his wife with no other means of support.

FERTILITY – JACK IN THE GREEN

The Celts celebrated May Day as Beltane. The Romans dedicated it to the Goddess Flora. At the start of spring, both cultures cut down a tree and covered it with garlands and ribbons. Thus originated the Maypole. Wild dances took place around it, with participants dressed up in costumes made from flowers and leaves. The prize of a silver crown was given for the most elaborate costume.

By the late 18th century, Working Men's guilds from far and wide were taking part in the competitions. The crown was won most frequently by the chimney sweeps, whose bodies were covered in foliage from head to foot entirely and which led to them being affectionately known as the Green

Men. The Green Man has been with civilisation in some form or other for thousands of years and is the embodiment of natural fertility.

In Hastings in Sussex, the winner was known as Jack in the Green and his behaviour upon winning was notoriously raucous and drunken. When Parliament put a stop to boys climbing chimneys in 1889, the ceremony was toned down until it became little more than a village fete.Since the 1970s the ceremony has been revived all over the country and survives to this day in such places as Whitstable and Rochester (both in Kent), Hastings, Bristol, Oxford, Castleton, Knutsford, Deptford, Greenwich, Bermondsey and at the Pagan Pride parade in Holborn, London.

The cult of the Green Man has also spread to America where it continues to grow. It is also celebrated in popular culture: in 2003, Suggs, frontman of the band Madness, was inspired by the Green Man he saw in Whitstable to write a song with Jools Holland called 'Jack O'The Green'.

FERTILITY SYMBOLS

Human beings have always had a natural fascination with the fundamentals of procreation. It took our ancestors many thousands of years to figure the ins and outs of childbearing. Gods were assumed to control the mysterious origin of babies.Various symbols of fertility were created to encourage these whimsical gods to smile favourably on couples intent on raising progeny.

Marriage has always been connected with fertility. The Mesopotamian Akitu (New Year's Festival) had close connections with *hieros gamos* ('sacred marriage') and in ancient Mesopotamia they made clay dolls smeared with menstrual blood.

In India, terracotta elephants were offered to the gods at weddings because elephants always gathered where it rained and rain is important for crops. Peacocks beat a tattoo with their feet when it rains, so they too became fertility symbols in India. The intricate paisley pattern is copied from mankolam (mango design) as it is known in Tamil, or ambi in Punjabi. Introduced into Europe by the East India Company in the 17th century, the mango and the lotus flower, fertility symbols, can be traced back to the legend of Brahma, who created the world while sitting on a lotus blossom.

The Hindus saw lotus flowers growing beautifully in the dirtiest of muddy waters and immediately imbued the lotus plant with fertile powers. Even the Buddhists who, one assumes, are self-possessed, have fertility gods such as Vajradhara-Shakti and Chakrasamvara-Vajravarahi.

Another symbol of fertility is the cat. The Egyptians even mummified their cats and sometimes were buried with them. Frogs too, being associated with water, were worshipped in ancient Egypt and Greece. Even in South America, the Aztecs worshipped frogs and toads as mother goddesses.

According to the Venerable Bede in a pamphlet called *De Temporum Ratione* in the eighth century, the pagan goddess of spring was called Oestre. Spring is associated with hares and rabbits and eggs. Easter is an anglicisation of Oestre.

When Celts still inhabited Ireland, they strung hazelnuts together to symbolise fertility. By the way, hazelnuts have an oil in them which is supposed to be particularly good to regulate insulin levels and blood pressure. Maybe it has other rousing effects.

Druids had a thing about mistletoe because it appears to be able to grow anywhere without discernible roots. They also believed it to be an aphrodisiac (which started the custom of us holding it above our heads and waiting to be kissed). In fact, mistletoes contain poisons such as phoratoxin and the alkaloid tyramine. Ingesting them can result in sickness and possibly death.

The Chinese saw the profusion of red seeds inside a pomegranate and immediately put that fruit down on the list of fertility symbols. They too are keen on elephants. They often keep a pair of china elephants either side of the bed. Fish breed a lot too. So, for their symbolic quality, fish are kept in bedrooms as well as in Chinese restaurants.

In Polynesia and, in particular, among the Maoris of New Zealand they have 'tiki'. Tiki is a small carved fellow in humanoid shape and he is not only a lucky charm but the personification of the first procreative act. The legend is this. Tiki was alone looking into a pond and saw his reflection. Thinking it was someone with whom he could play, he jumped in, but his reflection disappeared. In a fit of pique he filled in the pond but out of the mud a creature formed, half-fish, half-woman. Tiki played with her and for some years he enjoyed the companionship of this creature. One day, in the pond which had reformed, an eel surfaced and touched the woman. The electrical charge passed to Tiki, and before he knew it, he was performing the pro-creative act with his lady friend. Tiki must have been a natural – look at how many people there are in the southern hemisphere now. People in New Zealand are encouraged to wear a little green tiki round their necks, and their optimism seems to be paying off.

In England, we have borrowed fertility symbols from all over the world. One of our indigenous symbols is too big to easily export. In the countryside in Dorset, on the A352 road just north of Cerne Abbas, is a vast giant sculpted out of the chalk hillside, representing a naked, club-wielding fellow in a state of sexual arousal. He is 55 metres (180 ft) high and 51 metres (167 ft) wide. Some say he is a Roman depiction of Hercules. And who is to deny it? Families driving through the West Country with a granny in the back sometimes take a wide detour to avoid the area near Dorchester.

And there you have it, a whole bunch of fertility symbols: eggs and bunnies and pomegranates. Could it all be one enormous fallacy?

Chapter 8

Afterplay

THE FIRST DANCE

In Britain it is traditional for the bride and groom to lead the proceedings and have the first dance at the celebratory reception or wedding breakfast. Some sources suggest that this custom stems from an ancient ritual wherein a woman (the bride) was stolen from her own tribe and hidden away in foreign territory. The kidnapper (the groom) would half-carry, half-drag his new woman around his own tribe in order to show her off and, in particular, to claim primary conjugal rights. These days, the first dance serves exactly the same purpose.

After the first dance, all the guests are invited to join in on the dance floor. The groom will dance with his new mother-in-law and then with his mother while the bride does the honours with her father-in-law and then her father.

Elsewhere in this book it is stated that in olden days families tried to marry off their oldest daughter first. If a younger daughter got hitched first, her older sister had to dance barefoot as a sort of penance. In Shakespeare's *The Taming of the Shrew*, one aspect of Katherine's shrewishness is highlighted by her fear that Bianca, her younger sister, might beat her to the altar. Kate spells it out: '...[if Bianca marries before her] I must dance barefoot on her wedding day.'

WEDDING BREAKFASTS

Historically, weddings were morning affairs. The celebratory meal would start at what we would call today brunch-time.

Canonical law decreed that marriages could only take place from eight o'clock in the morning until mid-day. However, since 1934, with dispensation extended until 6pm, the ceremonies have crept into the afternoons. The bun fights tend to start in the early evening. Everyone continues to call these raucous occasions 'wedding breakfasts'. Perhaps, in time, the name will change to 'wedding cocktails'.

After Edward VIII abdicated so he would be free to marry Wallis Simpson, they had their wedding breakfast in Paris. The Duke of Windsor, as he was retitled, had such a penchant for Scottish kippers and Seville marmalade that for the breakfast he had them shipped to him from Fortnum & Mason in Piccadilly.

HONEYMOONS

In antiquity there were some cultures in which a marriage could only take place under a full moon. There are several theories as to the possible origins of the word 'honeymoon'. Some regard the word 'moon' as referring to the full moon because in ancient times, Teutonic weddings were held when the moon was full.

This chronicler prefers the notion that 'moon' is a corruption of the word 'month'. In pagan times, when the woman was kidnapped and taken into captivity, it would have taken about a month to ensure she was impregnated. Once this had happened, her own tribe would abandon the hunt and disinherit her. Then the new husband could relax and settle down to start his own dynasty with his pregnant wife.

Being on the run for the better part of a month, the choice

of food was limited to the staples of the times – honey and mead being among the basic foodstuffs available. It seems possible that for the first month of enforced marriage the couple existed on a meagre but high-energy diet.

The first use of the word appeared in the 16th century, though in that era it did not refer to a vacation. Couples were expected to remain chaste until marriage. The honeymoon was simply a time for them to become acclimatised to a more physical relationship. The inclusion of a secluded tryst grew to be part of the tradition later, first practised by the leisured classes in the Regency period. It was not until the 20th century that it gained common ground amongst the general public.

There are other theories regarding the etymology of the word 'honeymoon', for example 'hymeneal', which is not only a wedding song but a word once used to mean consummation of marriage (the hymen being broken). Whatever the root, honeymooners have always aspired to find some cosy hideaway where they can bill and coo in private.

BED

Only one thing can seal the marriage contract officially, and that is consummation; 'non-consummation' is grounds for divorce. Although not essential, consummation usually takes place in a bed.

In the atrium or tablinum of a typical villa in ancient Rome there would be enthroned the symbolic bed as a reminder that the wife of the house was destined to be a mother. The marriage was only considered fully consummated once the first child was born.

Until the 18th century, churches often provided 'a wedding house' that included a bedchamber specifically designed to cater for consummation. The newly-weds would have been given little privacy.

Royal weddings are most fully documented. In Tudor times (1485–1603) the routine was first, for the Bishop and his chaplains to bless the bed before the royal couple got into it. Second, the newly-weds drank a special nightcap known as 'the Benediction posset' specially mixed for them. Also blessed, it consisted of sweetened, spiced wine. No doubt the celibate priests considered that consummation needed some sustenance.

In those weddings where the monarch had married a virgin (as opposed to a widow) it was considered important to prove to the world that the bride was deflowered on her wedding night. Crowds assembled in the courtyards below the bedrooms of newly married royals. Come the dawn, the window was flung open and the blood-stained sheet held up and displayed to the mob as proof that the deed had been done, that the hymen had been breached and that their new queen was now a fully fledged woman. Of course, if the lady in question had not lived an unsullied existence she would have had a suitable sheet smuggled in beforehand. Gossip has percolated down through the centuries suggesting that many a wife on her wedding night resorted to subterfuge.

GROUNDS FOR ANNULMENT

At the time of a marriage there are several reasons that can cause it to be challenged, and most couples can apply later in married life for an annulment. They include, consanguinity, fraud, undue influence, duress, improper age, mental incompetence, bigamy and lack of consent. Incestuous marriages are those between a couple related by full or half-blood. Consanguinity includes brothers and sisters, first cousins, uncles and nieces, grandparents and grandchildren and parents and grandchildren.

DIVORCE – TILL DEBT DO US PART

Statistics are a variable feast. Figures written at the time of this book's publication may change totally in another couple of years. For what it is worth, the Office for National Statistics for England and Wales informs us that in 2011, 117,558 couples decided to shed the yoke permanently. This represented a reduction of 3 per cent over five years. It is mooted that the overwhelming reason for a declining divorce rate is financial. Divorce is an expensive business, both monetarily and emotionally. These statistics bolster the cautionary note sounded in the old adage, 'marry in haste – repent at leisure'.

The only age group to record an annual increase in the number of divorces are those in the mature 50–59 category (more than 23,000 couples). Committing oneself to marriage seems to be approached with more caution as time goes by. In the 10 years up until 2011, the number of couples declaring themselves to be cohabiting jumped 30 per cent to 2.3 million.

In the United States, marriages don't necessarily go on till death do them part. An American couple will remain married, on average, just 11 years. The divorce rate is between 3.5 and 4 divorces per 1,000 people, amounting to upwards of 900,000 divorces per year. Even so, most marriages last for life because family values really do matter. The traditional 'nuclear' family consists of a man, his wife and 2.4 children. (It is the consequences of divorce on the life of that point fourth of a child that many observers worry about.)

In the UK, each divorce will set back the petitioner an

average of £1,300 (according to the Government-sponsored leaflet *The Price of Separation*). Formerly it was possible to apply for legal aid in divorce cases where the applicants were on benefits, but since April 2013, this is no longer available.

Before 1857, it was necessary to secure an Act of Parliament to annul a marriage. After the Matrimonial Causes Act it became possible to apply for civil divorce. The Matrimonial Causes Act of 1937, which was introduced by the novelist AP Herbert, MP, extended the grounds for divorce to include desertion for over three years, cruelty and incurable insanity.

In 1969, the Divorce Reform Act added yet another extenuating circumstance for divorce: marital breakdown by mutual consent. It also removed the necessity for either partner to prove the other at fault in order to end the marriage.

Currently there are six basic grounds for divorce. They are:

1. Desertion
2. Cruelty and unreasonable behaviour
3. Insanity
4. Adultery
5. A signed declaration that the couple has lived apart for more than two years
6. Having lived apart for more than five years.

As regards cruelty, in 1976, following pressure by the women's movement, the Domestic Violence and Matrimonial Proceedings Act was introduced. This provided legal protection to female victims of domestic violence.

The person applying for a divorce is known as 'the

petitioner' and is liable for the court costs, which at the time of writing are £340. The partner who is being discarded is known as 'the respondent'. He or she will be served with a divorce petition from the court. This should cost nothing unless the divorce is being contested in which case the court charges a fee of £230. If both parties agree to the divorce, the judge will issue a decree nisi, meaning that mutual agreement has been reached. There is then a 'cooling down' period of six weeks. If no reconciliation is forthcoming, a decree absolute can be issued declaring the marriage null and void. This costs £45. Solicitors' fees vary but an uncontested divorce with minimal complications will cost in the region of £750–£1000. The fees can be intimidating, not to say prohibitive, and if a financial settlement cannot be reached without mediation, a cheaper service is obtainable online: resolution.org.uk.

A VINCULO MATRIMONII

According to *Black's Law Dictionary*, 'divorce a vinculo matrimonii' is a total divorce of husband and wife, dissolving the marriage tie, and releasing the parties wholly from their matrimonial obligations: a divorce from the bond of marriage.

BILL OF DIVORCEMENT

The expression was coined in the Bible in the Book of Jeremiah (3:8). Interpreted in the version of the World English Bible as: 'I saw, when, for this very cause that backsliding Israel had committed adultery, I had put her away and given her a bill of divorce, yet treacherous Judah, her sister, didn't fear; but she also went and played the prostitute.'

This is not to be confused with a stage play called *A Bill of Divorcement* by Clemence Dane, which was adapted into a film by George Cukor in 1932, starring Katharine Hepburn and John Barrymore.

WEDDING ANNIVERSARIES

We owe the concept of giving tokens for certain wedding anniversaries to our old friends, the Romans. When the Emperor Constantine converted to Christianity in AD 313, he gave the citizens of Rome another excuse not merely to talk of their love but to express it with physical gifts. Husbands crowned their wives with silver wreaths on their 25th anniversaries and gold wreaths on the 50th.

In the English-speaking world, there is a growing convergence of agreement regarding anniversary symbols, including flowers, precious gems and the giving of particular titles to anniversaries. For example, a first anniversary used to be called the 'paper anniversary' in Europe, but now 'cotton anniversary' is largely accepted.

In 1838, Charles Dickens published *Nicholas Nickleby*, in which he refers to an eighth wedding anniversary (Chapter 14), which indicates these celebrations have been seriously observed for a considerable time.For centuries, the only anniversaries that had a gift associated with them were the 1st, 5th, 10th, 15th, 20th, 25th, 50th and 75th anniversaries. Then, in 1937, the American National Retail Jewelers' Association (ANRJA) realised they were missing a trick. The organisation (now called Jewelers of America) manufactured a much longer list of gifts covering many more anniversaries and subtly promoting the following list:

Anniversary	Theme
First	Paper
Second	Cotton
Third	Leather
Fourth	UK: Flower/Fruit US: Linen/Silk
Fifth	Wooden
Sixth	UK: Sugar US: Iron
Seventh	Woollen
Eighth	Bronze
Ninth	UK: Copper/Willow US:Pottery
Tenth	Tin
Eleventh	Steel
Twelfth	UK: Fine Linen US: Silk
Thirteenth	Lace
Fourteenth	Ivory
Fifteenth	Crystal
Sixteenth	Porcelain
Twentieth	China
Twenty-fifth	Silver
Thirtieth	Pearl
Thirty-fifth	Coral
Fortieth	Ruby
Forty-fifth	Sapphire
Fiftieth	Golden
Fifty-fifth	Emerald
Sixtieth	Diamond
Sixty-fifth	Blue Sapphire
Seventieth	Platinum
Seventy-fifth	Diamond and Gold
Eightieth	Oak
Eighty-fifth	Wine

The 60th-anniversary token was not originally a diamond, but after Queen Victoria had sat for 60 years on the British throne, the celebration was given the title of 'Diamond Jubilee'. That is the reason why 'gold' was hastily conjured up as an additional extra for the 75th wedding anniversary.

British subjects attaining the age of 100 receive a telegram from the reigning monarch. In Commonwealth countries, if requested, a congratulatory message can be received from Buckingham Palace for 60th, 65th and 70th wedding anniversaries. In Canada and Australia, one can request a message from the Governor General for the 50th anniversary, and every fifth anniversary after that.

The President of the United States will send a greeting to anyone attaining a 50th wedding anniversary, although it is unlikely he keeps a note of these occasions in his personal diary.

The Pope can be requested to dispense a Papal Blessing document to all those Roman Catholics celebrating 25th, 50 and 60th wedding anniversaries through their local diocese.

THRESHOLD

There is a folk myth that 'thresh' was a bar or a block of wood that held down the chaff-and-sawdust flooring. This is erroneous: 'thresh' has always been a verb, as in 'to thresh wheat'; it has never been a noun. 'Threshold' comes from Old English (*brescan*) meaning 'to tread' or 'to trample'. The origin of 'hold' is unknown but the best guess is it means 'sill' or 'frame'. In other words, a threshold is the frame through which one crosses to get out of a room or to go in – any gateway. So when the groom carries his bride over the threshold (the archaic symbolism for which is discussed in Carrying the bride over the threshold, page 129) it means merely he is transporting her through the gateway to heavenly bliss.

It was expected of the bride that she should display a modest reluctance as she was carried over the threshold.

RENEWAL OF MARRIAGE VOWS

There can be a number of reasons why couples opt for a renewal of their marriage vows. Sometimes, it is to celebrate a special wedding anniversary, and they want to let everyone know how many happy years they've had together. Or if the original marriage took place abroad, the couple may want to renew the vows in front of family and friends. Sometimes a couple may wish to put the strain of difficult times behind them and re-commit to each other.

William Shakespeare summed up the whole thing rather neatly in his famous 'Sonnet 116'. Here is an extract:

> …Love is not love which alters when it alteration finds,
> Or bends with the remover to remove.
> O, no! It is an ever-fixed mark that looks on tempests and is never shaken.
> It is the star to every wandering bark, whose worth's unknown, although his height be taken.
> Love's not Time's fool, though rosy lips and cheeks
> Within his bending sickle's compass come:
> Love alters not with his brief hours and weeks,
> But bears it out even to the edge of doom…

Vows can be renewed in civil ceremonies. Christians believe that marriage is a gift of God and they will generally renew their vows in church. This service is an opportunity for rejoicing and thanking God for a marriage. It is also meant as an encouragement to children and grandchildren that marriages can be the source of God's richest blessing, that marriage is a private undertaking but it has a public importance.

The service is the declaration of continuing love and devotion rather than a legal ceremony. The only condition placed upon those seeking this ceremony is that they are already legally married. It is recorded in the church register and a special church card presented to the couple, signed by the minister conducting the service, which is an affirmation of the strength of the married couple's love and faith in each other and in God. No wedding register is signed and there is no charge for a simple service with just a few witnesses and the minister present.

FORCED MARRIAGES

Traditionally, under Islamic Shari'a law, any wali (guardian) who is a blood relative of a girl, can force an underage virgin into marriage without her consent. The wali must be a *wali mujbir*, that is to say, the father or the paternal grandfather of the proposed bride. The marriage contract is sealed between the *wali mujbir* and the bridegroom's family and not between the bride and the groom.

More liberal proponents of Islam insist that 'forced marriages are strictly forbidden'. The problem is that a growing number of fundamentalists are not so liberal. Fundamentalists dispute whether such forced marriages performed against the expressed will of the girl can be declared void by the *Gadi* (authoritative power held by a village development committee) when she comes of age (see Arranged marriages, page 214).

CAXTON HALL

Caxton Hall served as the register office for more than 50,000 marriages. Located in central London, with a catchment area that included Belgravia and much of Mayfair, the last couple to be married there in the 1970s were Regina Dangerfield and Robert Clairborne-Dixon. The venue was famous for the number of celebrity marriages that took place there. Elizabeth Taylor, Peter Sellers, Roger Moore, Orson Welles and Ringo Starr were just the tip of the iced wedding cake.

Apart from hosting wedding ceremonies, in 1906, the suffragettes held their first meeting at Caxton Hall, and in 1910, the occultist Aleister Crowley celebrated the 'Rites of Eleusis' there. Performing these public invocations with him were Leila Waddell and Victor Neuberg. Allegedly, they brought the audience to a religious ecstasy.

During the Second World War, Winston Churchill gave press conferences from Caxton Hall. In the 1970s it was converted into a block of 13 luxury apartments, and no weddings have been held there since.

WIDOW'S WEEDS

After the Edwardian Conquest of Wales, the Statute of Rhuddlan (1284; it established the constitutional basis for government of the principality) perpetuated the long-held English custom of assigning a widow one third of the land held by her husband. In addition, she became entitled to the balance of the original settlement made to her at the church door by the bridegroom with the consent of his father. The word 'weeds' refers to the heavy, unrevealing black clothing which, from the 19th century, widows were expected to wear, and comes from Old English wæd, meaning garment.

MIDWIVES

The first royal midwife mentioned in historic documents is Margaret Cobbe who, in 1469, was granted an annual pension as midwife to the 32-year-old Queen of England, wife of the extremely tall Edward IV. (You'll find many interesting things about her in *The Book of Royal Useless Information*, also published by John Blake.)

King Edward had married the widow Elizabeth Wydville in secret at Stony Stratford near Northampton. She was the first commoner to marry a king since 1066. Her children included the so-called Princes in the Tower who both mysteriously vanished. Altogether, she had 12 children (two by a previous marriage).

Margaret Cobbe attended the Queen's fourth parturition at the birth of Edward, the elder of the little princes doomed to disappear. He was born in a gloomy building called the Sanctuary, near Westminster Palace, to which his mother had fled in panic while his father was away quelling a rebellion. The Queen had registered herself and her three daughters as Sanctuary women. She was 'destitute of every necessity for her confinement', but the Abbot of Westminster 'sent various conveniences' from the Abbey close by, and 'Mother Cobbe, a well-disposed midwife, charitably assisted the distressed queen in the hour of maternal peril and acted as nurse to the little prince', the much-hoped-for heir. When the rebellion was over, Edward IV bestowed 'princely rewards on the humble friends who had aided his Elizabeth, as he calls her, in that fearful crisis.' He pensioned Margaret Cobbe with £12 per annum, a generous sum for the age.

The population at large was slow to accept the need for midwives. A great deal of suspicion surrounded them even though they came from the ranks of senior women in the community and who were generally experienced married women who had given birth. Under a Church Act of 1512, laws were drawn up forbidding them 'to connive at contraception, abortion, child destruction or concealment of birth'. The midwife's duties were incorporated into the oath she swore under the licensing system operated through the Act.

In 1665, a book was published for the instruction of midwives called *The County Midwife's Opusculum or Vade Mecum*, but it was privately published, and did not appear in a more general edition until the following century. It showed, however, that the acceptance of midwives was gaining ground, and in 1902 the landmark Midwives Act came into force. Under a successor Act in 1936, provisions were drawn up for a nationwide service of midwives with salaries and pensions. Thus midwifery was officially recognised in law. In North America, the absence of legislature has meant that state-appointed midwives are becoming something of a rarity.

STAY-AT-HOME-HUSBANDS

The Office for National Statistics announced in 2013 that in Britain there are 227,000 stay-at-home 'house husbands'.

WORLD WEDDING STATISTICS

The number of weddings in the world every day is estimated at 115,000.

In China there are over 9,000,000 weddings per year, each costing on average $19,900.

In the USA there are more than 2,000,000 weddings every year.

The most popular month to marry in America is July. (As a matter of incidental interest, until the Victorian era, 'July' was pronounced by all to rhyme with 'truly'.)

The most popular wedding venues are: Las Vegas (92,000 weddings per annum); Istanbul, Turkey (91,000); Gatlinburg, Tennessee (42,000). The average number of guests invited to a wedding is 145.

In 2012, according to the Office for National Statistics in England and Wales, the proportion of children born out of wedlock or outside of a civil partnership reached a record 47.5 per cent. This was the first time since the census began in 1801 that married couples with children had been in a minority. Five million people live with a partner while remaining unmarried. One hundred and fifty thousand declared themselves living in civil partnerships. Accordingly, Prime Minister David Cameron promised extra tax breaks for married couples with children.

According to a survey carried out in 2013 by Slater & Gordon – a law firm – a third of all married women in the UK have at one time considered divorce, but the fear of financial or emotional hardship forces them to remain in loveless relationships.

LONGEST-LASTING MARRIAGES

At the time of writing (as of March 2013), the couple still living and enjoying the longest marriage are: Karan Chand (born 10 November 1905) who was married in December 1925 to Kartari Chand (born 1 November 1912). Still married after 87 years.

However, the longest marriage EVER recorded is:

David Frederick Bateman (9 October 1759 – 5 April 1869) who married Susan (née Brewer) Bateman (2 January 1758 – 10 September 1863) and married 29 August 1772. They had a marriage that lasted 91 years and 12 days. They lived in New York, New York, a wonderful town.

MASS WEDDINGS

The Holy Spirit Association for the Unification of World Christianity was a religious movement founded in 1954 in South Korea. It is commonly called the Unification Church and has spread throughout the world. Its founder, Mun Yong-Myong, claimed that Jesus appeared to him on 17 April 1935 and asked him to continue His work. After a period of reflection, Mun Yong-Myong agreed to take on the task and changed his name to Sun Myung Moon. He set about founding the new Order, which is sometimes referred to as 'the Moonies'.

At the age of 72, Sun Myung Moon declared that he and his wife, Hak Ja Han, were Messiahs. When Moon died on 3 September 2012, Mrs Moon and their sons, Hyung Jin Moon and Kook Jin Moon, took control of the Unification Church.

The movement has become famous for its mass weddings. In 1993, 20,825 couples were married in the Olympic Stadium in Seoul. Another 9,800 couples in 10 other countries were linked to the ceremony by satellite. Backing the Church are business enterprises including the Tongil Group – an empire with interests in publishing, property, schools and soft drinks. The word 'tongil' means 'unification' in Korean.

On 17 February 2013, South Korea's Unification Church held the first mass wedding since the death of its founder,

under the leadership of Hak Ja Han. The 7,000 participants from 70 countries exchanged wedding rings at the Cheongshim Peace Centre in Gapyeong, south of Seoul.

On a more modest scale, mass weddings have been recorded in the United Kingdom for centuries. Today they are more common in Muslim countries particularly among the Shia sects and are performed with increasing frequency. In Iraq, to celebrate Saddam Hussein's new term of office in 2002, 500 couples were married simultaneously. The concept continues to spread, as in the Nicaraguan capital of Managua where 550 couples married on St Valentine's Day, 2013.

It holds a particular appeal for those couples that don't have the money for a private wedding.

Chapter 9

For better, For worse

AFGHANISTAN

Afghanistan has no age of consent. The law of this country bans sex outside marriage. An ancient practice persists that stems from the social separation of men and women, of boys dressing as girls to entertain men. At the end, boys are auctioned for sexual exploitation. If caught, the boys are jailed.

AMISH WEDDINGS

In Martin Luther's wildest dreams, he could not have visualised the almighty rift in the Church that would result from nailing his 95 Theses, protesting against the venality of priests, to the door of Wittenberg Church in 1517. Catholics and Protestants have been fencing with each other ever since.

Early on, a third group joined the fray, calling themselves Anabaptists. They stood aloof from the Catholics and Protestants, and decided they could baptise themselves. In 1527, they categorised their beliefs in a document called *Brotherly Union*. The credo was simple and taught that the followers of Christ should be consistently honest, should refrain from using force and should maintain a loving heart towards their fellow man.

The group expanded and the followers became known as Mennonites, with a power base in Switzerland. Eventually, this group had internal differences of opinion and a breakaway sect was formed led by a man called Jacob

Amman. His followers were called Amish. Emigration to the New World followed, and today the centre of the Amish community is based in Pennsylvania.

Amish people are mainly farmers and they use traditional methods of agriculture. The laws of Amish, known as Ordnung, are largely orally conveyed and, since they have been recounted from generation to generation over 300 years, nearly everything is based on the lifestyle of the past. Belts, ties and gloves are forbidden. Moustaches are forbidden. Youths must remain clean-shaven, but after marriage men must let their beards grow. Hair must not be cut. Women cannot wear jewellery or patterned clothing.

Choosing a mate is limited to other members of the Amish church, and this has resulted in a degree of inbreeding over the generations. Baptism is an essential prerequisite to marriage. A newly married couple may expect to have built a new home for themselves on the family farm, which may well be commandeered by their spiritual brothers for Sunday service. Divorce is not unheard of but it is contrary to Amish church behaviour.

AUSTRALIA

Whereas in Europe a wedding has to take place in an officially designated building, in Australia, a wedding can be held anywhere. Traditions can spread quickly. Within living memory it has become customary in Australia for the wedding guests to tie silver horseshoes with ribbons on to the bride's wrists.

BERMUDA

North of Florida is the small island of Bermuda, a British dependency discovered in the 16th century where the island's reefs caused many a shipwreck. Sailors nicknamed it 'The Isle of Devils'. John Rolfe, who later went on to marry Pocahontas, was one of the few survivors of those who had been wrecked there. This may have inspired William Shakespeare to use the island and Rolfe's story as the setting for *The Tempest*.

To ensure that a newly betrothed couple grows old and prospers together, Bermudian couples top the bride's wedding cake (they often have his-and-hers desserts) with a tiny cedar sapling. They take the sapling home and plant it. Then they can watch it grow and mature – mirroring their own relationship. Often, two wedding cakes are made, one for the bride and one for the groom. One of the cakes is heavily laced with rum – is that for him or for her? Both cakes are placed in a heart-shaped wreath of ivy.

CHINA (SICHUAN PROVINCE)

In southwest China they follow an old tradition in which women are required to cry at weddings. This originated in about 300 BC when a princess of the Zhao State was to marry a prince of the Yan State. The story goes that as the bride left home to attend her wedding, her mother burst into tears, threw herself at her daughter's feet and begged her to come home as soon as possible. The daughter cried too and gave her promise. Today, amongst the Tujia people, it is compulsory for the bride and her close female relatives to cry at the wedding ceremony. What's more, the tears have to appear to be genuine.

In some regions the custom is called Zuo Tang. Every night for a month before the big day, the bride must attend a meeting hall where she has to cry for an hour. After a few days, her mother accompanies her, also crying. Within a week, her grandmother joins in, and eventually the rest of the women. A cacophony of wailing carries on, including the singing of traditional 'Crying Songs for Marriages'. There is a recorded instance of a bride being beaten to death for not crying properly.

As the day of the wedding gets closer, the women grow more animated and strident. They start swearing at the matchmaker (for nearly all marriages in China are arranged). By the time the ceremony takes place, the bride is washed-out and compliant. Perhaps this is a cunning ruse devised by wise, inscrutable Chinese men.

CONGO

It is considered undignified and an affront to the betrothed couple should anyone be witnessed smiling during the ceremony. Weddings must be treated with the utmost solemnity.

CZECHS ENDORSED

On the day prior to her wedding, many a Czech bride will find a newly planted tree in her back yard, festooned with colourful ribbons and painted eggshells. Tradition has it that the bride will live as long as the tree.

FIJI

When a young man asks a father for his daughter's hand in marriage, it is customary for the prospective bridegroom to present his future father-in-law with a whale's tooth. Perhaps the roots of this go back to a time when a prospective groom had to prove his prowess. It is certainly a lot to be asked of a young man nowadays, particularly with whales being a protected species. The trade in second-hand whale's teeth is understood to be brisk.

FRANCE

At the wedding reception it is usual for the newly-weds to drink wine from a special cup with two handles called a cup of marriage (*coup de mariage*). These can be elaborately tooled pieces. When the guests take their leave, they strew laurel leaves in their path.

Should the couple decide to stay at home instead of going away on a honeymoon, on their first night together the neighbours conduct a charivari ('rough music'). A crowd of well-wishers congregate outside the marital pad yelling encouraging remarks of a ribald nature and making as much din as possible with pots and pans. At a suitable juncture, the newly-weds emerge sheepishly giving the impression that consummation has been accomplished, and the guests are sent away with bottles of wine.

French law requires the posting of marriage banns at the appropriate city hall (*mairie*) no less than 10 days preceding the date set for the wedding.

In France, it is legally compulsory to have a civil ceremony before any religious celebration. Marriages cannot be performed in embassies but must be performed by an *officier de l'etat civil*. In practice, this includes the mayor (*maire*) or the deputy mayor (*adjoint*) or an appointed town councillor (*conseiller municipal*).

In France a religious ceremony does not constitute a legal marriage. A religious ceremony may be performed after (never before) the civil ceremony. The minister, priest or rabbi performing the religious ceremony requires the proof of a certificate of civil marriage.

INDIA

In Hindi, toe rings are called *bichiya*. In Telugu, they are *mettelu*, and in Tamil, *metti*. In a land where sandals are the norm, toe rings are worn to indicate that the wearer is a married person. Normally silver, they are worn on the second toe of each foot.

THE INUIT (ESKIMOS)

The Inuit lay claim to being the original Native Americans. Until Christianity was introduced to them in the early part of the 20th century, there were no real marriage traditions apart from the strict custom that a man should always marry outside his tribe (exogamy).

The prospective groom would bond with the bride's father and become his hunting partner for about a year, after which the daughter would move to the groom's home. Wives were sometimes shared between hunters (*nangsaghag*) although this was rare. If an older brother died, the wife would be taken on by the younger brother, who would also take full responsibility for any earlier offspring.

Divorce was informal. After a disagreement or if the wife was homesick, she would simply return to her parents who would resume taking care of her. Inuits live in an extremely cold climate and therefore their bodies are thickly covered most of the time, often leaving just their eyes and their noses exposed. Thus they express greeting and affection by means of a '*kunik*'. This involves pressing one's nose against another's nose and breathing in – sometimes referred to as 'the Eskimo kiss'.

In modern times the Inuits follow the Christian practice of exchanging marriage vows, and they have developed their own wedding prayer:

You are my husband, you are my wife
My feet shall run because of you
My feet dance because of you
My heart shall beat because of you
My eyes see because of you
My mind thinks because of you
And I shall love, because of you.

On a completely different topic, the phrase 'pissed as a newt' is allegedly a mispronunciation. When the Inuit first met the adventurers from the West, they were offered alcohol as a gift in exchange for furs and sealskin. The Inuit had never come across alcohol before and they became wildly drunk after the first couple of swigs. The story of their limited tolerance and innocence soon spread to Europe. But the expression 'pissed as an Inuit' meant little in common parlance and the word 'Inuit' was soon changed to 'newt'.

IRELAND

At the wedding reception, when the husband takes his new wife onto the floor for the first dance, her feet must always be in contact with the floor. In the 'land of the little people', the superstition still holds sway that if the bride takes both feet off the ground, she will be light enough for the fairies to whisk her away. Sorcery, leprechauns and black magic all represent tangible threats in the subconscious of modern society.

ITALY

After a wedding ceremony in Italy, tradition flourishes at the reception. Called *il buste*, the bride carries a satin purse called a *borsa* and the female guests are expected to fill it with dainty packages containing cash. The men also contribute, but in return they request a dance with the bride. While that is going on, the grandmother, left alone and being an old hand at the task, may use less subtle arm-twisting methods to fill the purse.

During the wedding feast, another local custom takes place. The groom's tie is cut off and chopped into little pieces. The groom auctions off each piece of tie for money, all of which goes into *la borsa*.

Finally, the newly-weds shatter a vase. Someone counts the pieces and this number represents how many years of married bliss lie ahead of them.

KENYA

Masai marriages are jolly affairs. After the marriage ceremony, the father of the bride blesses his daughter and leaves his DNA on her hair and her breasts by spitting on her before she goes off with her husband to start a new life.

KOREA

In Korea, just because the wedding ceremony is over that doesn't mean the newly married man can vamp till ready. Before he can leave the reception, his best men and other cohorts waylay him in the kindest possible way: they remove his shoes and socks, tie his ankles together, and begin beating him on the soles of his feet with a dried, yellow corvina fish, a species that can grow up to three feet in length. During the event, he is subjected to an interrogation and if he answers the questions unsatisfactorily, the beating can become severe. The ritual is called *falaka* or *bastinado*. Bizarre as it may seem, this procedure is deemed to be the secret to acclimatising a new husband to his first night of matrimony.

MARQUESAS ISLANDS

These consist of 14 islands in French Polynesia. Following the marriage ceremony, the bride's relatives lie face down on the ground, in a closely compacted group. The newly-weds walk over everybody as they cross this human carpet on the way to their new life. This may be their last chance in life to walk over people.

MAURITANIA

In Mauritania, in West Africa, the worth of a marriageable woman is decided by her weight – the fatter the better. It is common for ladies of marriageable age to go to a special nursing home to be fattened up for eligibility.

MEXICO

Pearls are not permitted at weddings. Mexicans believe that pearls represent tears, and that if a bride wears them on her wedding day, she is bound to have an unhappy marriage. Sometimes a 'lasso' formed of white ribbon is tied round the necks of the bride and groom, in a symbolic joining (*padrinos de lazo*).

Christ together with his 12 apostles represents a symbolic number, so the groom gives his bride 13 coins (*arras*). These are blessed by the priest and signify the husband's willingness to provide for his bride.

MOROCCO

Inhabiting the area around the Tafilalet oasis in the south-east of Morocco is the Muslim Berber tribe of Ait Atta. When a bride of one of these clans gets married, she has to have her face covered with a red silk scarf throughout the three days of the ceremony. Nobody is allowed to see her face except the groom.

NATIVE AMERICANS

The Navajo

During the marriage ceremony, a Navajo couple stand side by side facing east, symbolising a new dawn. The Navajos wear colourful clothes for the occasion: black for the north, blue for the south, orange for the west and white for the east.

The Cherokee

Among the Cherokee, the mother has final approval on the choice of a husband for any of her daughters. A marriage might be arranged at the age of eight, but it would not be consummated until the girl was at least 15. In old Cherokee culture, everything was owned in the name of the woman – the home, the goods, even the children.

It was forbidden for unmarried girls to look directly into the eyes of a man, with the exception of men in their immediate families.

Before a date for marriage could be made, the oldest medicine man in the village had to be consulted. He would make a test for witches and examine the health of the couple before pronouncing whether they were compatible.

Once the approval of the Elders had been obtained, the wedding party would meet in a council chamber, the women lined up on one side of the room and the men on the other. The Basket Ceremony was enacted. The bride's mother would bring in a basket of corn and bread and a blanket and the groom's mother a basket of cooked meat and a blanket. The bride and groom would approach other and take the baskets into the centre of the room. For the first time, the bride would look directly into the eyes of her man. They would then join blankets and share the food. The head man would formally announce that the blankets were now joined, and the wedding was over. Prayers were made to the Great Spirit.

The Sioux

In former days, chastity for unmarried women was so important that women were not allowed to look into the eyes of strange men. The Sioux culture demanded that fathers negotiated their daughters' marriages.

A Sioux brave with an eye on a particular girl might buy a love potion from a Cree medicine man, but these could be mixtures of strange herbs with human hair and elk horn. Medicines such as these were by no means infallible, and they frequently made the suitor sick.

When the groom's mother and her relatives started to build him a new lodge made from elk skin, it was a signal to the rest of the village that a marriage had been agreed upon and the wedding date was imminent. The groom's dowry to his bride would usually be in horses – depending on his standing, anything between two to six. On rare occasions, up to 40 horses have been offered.

On the morning of the ceremony, half a dozen drummers would beat out a rhythm while the women danced and cooked. Eating and cooking continued throughout the day. Four men would take hold of the corners of a big blanket and held it aloft – similar to the canopy in a Jewish wedding – and the bride and groom and their close friends stood under it. The oldest medicine man would go to the front and lead a parade, marching to drums, through the village.

The officiating Chief would be arrayed in full paint and feathers. He held a staff of green ash with which he conducted the ceremony. He praised the pair and proclaimed them joined together as man and wife. The newly-weds would lead their party to the freshly built elk skin lodge and there the nuptial celebrations would continue until the following dawn.

POLAND

The bride and groom arrive at the church simultaneously and walk down the aisle together followed by the best man and the bridesmaids. The best man has little to do other than act as one of the witnesses and collect the paper money, which is given by the guests after the ceremony is over.

Prior to the ceremony, the wedding ring is given for safe-keeping to the priest. After the service is over, as the newly-weds leave the church, they are showered with small change. It is an essential part of the tradition that the couple stoop to retrieve the coins. Once this humiliation is over, they are given packages of paper money – 200 to 400 zloty (£40 –£80) per envelope.

Only those guests who have been invited to the *wesele* (riotous festivity) continue to the reception where vodka is provided in industrial quantities. The parents greet the couple with salt and bread and a goblet of wine. One of them will say, 'In accordance with our Polish traditions we greet you with bread and salt so that your home will always be safe and you may never be hungry.' Salt was believed to drive away evil spirits; wine to quench the thirst.

Once the bride and groom have eaten a slice of bread, they smash the plate and goblet on the floor, which is the cue to replenish the vodka glasses. Singing is traditional, starting with 'Sto Lat' ('One hundred years'). This is sung at most Polish celebrations from birthdays to Christmas.

Not until the height of the festivities does the bride throw her bouquet. The older people melt away at this point and leave things to proceed under the auspices of the youngsters. Courses of food go on being served all night. Polish weddings continue for two or three days, with the second day known as the '*poprawiny*'.

PUERTO RICO

The bouquet carried by the bride in Puerto Rico consists of poppy flowers (called *amapolas* in Spanish), which are symbolic of good fortune. In addition, she may carry a flamboyantly decorated fan.

Placed on the table at the wedding reception is a doll made in the image of the bride. Stuck into this doll are pins called *capias*, which are removed and used by the guests to pin money onto the bride's dress.

SHAMANIC WEDDINGS

Throughout the world, among those who reject monotheism, is a branch of Pagan worship that continues to be popular known as shamanism.

A shaman priest liaises between our physical and the spiritual world. The practitioners of shamanism believe they can call upon spirit guides, such as the spirits of ancestors, nature and animals. It is believed that physical and mental illnesses can be counterbalanced by calling upon such spiritual forces. Someone seeking help must meet the spirits halfway by going into an altered state of consciousness. Drumming and singing can help this transformation to take place.

Some shamanic churches have achieved official recognition. There is, for example, the group known as 'The Circle of the Sacred Earth', which customises wedding ceremonies to reflect a couple's spiritual needs. There is no fixed agenda for a shamanic wedding and each practitioner can add or subtract elements according to the individual needs of the bride and groom. The couple may write their own vows and subsume Christian aspects if needs be.

To meet the spirits, a couple must prepare themselves by means of meditation or yoga. When the ceremony begins, the guests gather in a circle holding hands. They invoke the presence of the spirits – ancestral spirits as well as those associated with the present company. The wedding party should be barefoot, allowing closer contact with Mother Earth. Offerings of grain or rice may be made to the spirits.

Among the rituals performed by a shaman priest during a marriage are handfasting (tying together the wrists of the couple during the vows, see page 103), limpia (infusing the air with dried leaves of the Peruvian chacapa plant), drum blessing (summoning the spirits through drums and song), blessing of the rings (invoking the spirit of Mother Earth to bless the rings) and pipe blessing (a sacred North American peace pipe is smoked to bring tranquillity to the union).

SPAIN

Spain is a country that follows the Catholic rituals regarding marriage, but it retains its Moorish background to lend colour to the ceremony. Arabs introduced oranges into Spain from Persia a thousand years ago, and the colour orange is predominant at Spanish weddings. Orange blossom is the national symbol of everlasting love in Spain. Brides wear orange blossoms in their hair and the bouquet is often composed of orange blossoms.

In order to be legally married in Spain it is necessary for at least one of the couples to be registered as a resident in the diocese of the Catholic church where the wedding is to take place.

SWEDEN

To ensure that their daughter will always be provided for, the parents of Swedish brides give her a special gift before the ceremony. Traditionally, the bride's mother places a gold coin in her daughter's right shoe and her father places a silver coin in her left shoe just before the wedding, symbolising that she'll never go without. Sometimes, though, this causes her to limp a bit.

TONGA WEDDINGS

In Tonga the making of 'tapa cloth' is important and significant. Tapa is made from the bark of the mulberry tree (*tutu*). At a Tongan wedding, tapa cloth is presented to the in-laws of both parties. The bed (*mohenga mole*), built specially for the honeymoon, is made of tapa cloth, as are the blankets (*kafu*).

Christianity is deeply embedded in Tongan culture and to get married requires residency for at least a month. Beach weddings are prohibited.

Royal marriages are spectacular affairs. The first one for 65 years took place in July 2012 when Tongan Crown Prince Tupouto'a 'Ulukalala married. Two thousand guests attended. All royal marriages are arranged, and members of the royal family may only marry other royal family members.

WELSH RARE BITS

Many of the traditional Welsh wedding customs such as the concealment of the bride, the race of the bride and bridegroom on horseback to and from the church pursued by young men, and the bidding letter (see Biddings, page 93) are extinct. Some remaining pranks include the holding-up of the procession by stretching rope across the road or by tying up the church gate, with the customary payment for release. If the couple is popular, an arch of evergreens will have been constructed over the church gate in anticipation of the ceremony.

In parts of western Wales some of the old customs still abound. On the morning of a wedding, the bridegroom and his posse call at the bride's home but the bride's mother and her friends bar their entry. This results in a great deal of good-natured banter and scuffling until the groom manages to get into the house. There, he will find the bride but she will be heavily disguised as an old granny clutching a baby doll. After a mock fight and much cajolery, she will allow herself to be 'captured' and led away by the groom's companions to the ceremony. On arrival at the chapel or the registry office, the wedding party will be confronted by the father of the bride who will 'rescue' his daughter and make off with her, pursued by the groom.

Eventually, the bride is caught and brought back to where the wedding is to take place, and the ceremony carries on in the traditional way. Without being aware of its significance, perhaps, the participants are echoing the old days of 'marriage by capture'.

NEWSPAPER ANNOUNCEMENTS

A localised custom in Knutsford, Cheshire was for the neighbours to make patterns in white sand outside the doors of the bride and of the groom.

Extract from the *Worcester Herald* 8 July 1707:

> Married. – Lately, Mr. Laley, of Acton, in Cheshire, aged 74, to Miss Coffin, of Whitchurch, Shropshire, aged 23. Seventy-four and a coffin cannot be an ill-timed match.

Another newspaper in April 1815, wrote that:

> William Jones, a pauper, aged 79, who has been married only three weeks, sold his wife for three-half-pence in the market place at Llanrwst.
>
> (Both from *Bye-Gones: Collected from old volumes of folklore* by Richard Holland, 1992)

Another superstition suggested it was unwise for a couple to hear their own banns called, 'lest the firstborn child be deaf and dumb'. Optimism seemed a rare commodity in those days.

PRISON MARRIAGES

In the United Kingdom, an application from a remand (unconvicted) prisoner to marry must immediately be referred to the local office of the Crown Prosecution Service (CPS) to see if there are any objections to the marriage taking place. Normally, any objection will be on the grounds that it may be a ruse by the defendant to obstruct the course of justice by marrying a witness.

Once a custodial prisoner's eligibility to marry has been confirmed, it is necessary to decide whether to hold the wedding inside the establishment – under the provisions of the Marriage Act 1983, unless it is a marriage according to the usages of the Jews or the Society of Friends (Quakers).

Most prisoners prefer a ceremony outside the establishment and sympathetic consideration is given to this whilst taking into account security and other public protection issues. Prisoners who are Category A, Provisional Category A, Restricted Status – or on the Escape List – must not be allowed to marry outside.

Operational managers, equivalent to a governor grade, should normally oversee arrangements for marriages taking place in prison. However, it is for prisoners to make all necessary arrangements with the superintendent segistrar and/or the relevant faith chaplain in consultation with the co-coordinating chaplain.

In the US, all prisoners have the constitutional right to marry. However, prison administrators are allowed to use their own discretion. In order to qualify for consideration, the inmate must be sentenced to a term less than life imprisonment, or be a 'life-termer' on parole. The prospective spouse must not be another prisoner or a close relative. The applicant must be over the legal age of consent, be mentally competent and seen to be acting voluntarily. The applicant cannot have a living spouse, nor be subject to any current, disciplinary hearings. Marriages are not permitted between prisoners of the same sex except (at the time of writing) in Massachusetts.

Conjugal Visits

Only 6 States allow conjugal visits in prison: California, Connecticut, Mississippi, New Mexico, New York and Washington. A long prison sentence for married prisoners in the other States does not come with much hope for marital consummation.

Marrying houses

At London's notorious Fleet Prison (known as the Fleet), the earliest recorded marriage of a prisoner was in 1613. Once called 'The Gaol of London', the Fleet was sited where lower Farringdon Street is today. An astonishing number of unlawful marriages were conducted there, officiated by unfrocked clergymen for under a guinea. The taverns in that area of London became known as 'marrying houses'. Women and young girls could be plied with gin or drugged and duped into pseudo-marriages.

Women seeking murderers

It's a curious thing how incarceration can attract certain women. Perhaps it's a mothering instinct or a quiet despair at the hopelessness of finding an ordinary, decent man. Take the following examples: Ted Bundy, mass murderer – killed 30 women over 5 years – received dozens of proposals of marriage before he met his end in the electric chair at Raiford Prison in Starke, Florida in 1989. Scott Peterson suffocated his wife and unborn child on Christmas Eve, 2002. He was convicted and sent to San Quentin State Prison in 2004. He is, at the time of writing, still in prison and still appealing against conviction. Even so, in the past 10 years, women from all over the world have proposed marriage to him.

One American State – Hawaii – has stonewalled on marriage for incarcerated criminals. When the State Government receives a request, it responds along the following lines:

> As ward of the State incarcerated in a correctional facility, you are incapable of providing the necessary emotional, financial and physical support that every marriage needs in order to succeed. We believe that for a healthy relationship, effort is required to make a marriage work. At this time while you are established in prison and unable to work and communicate effectively face to face with your fiancée, acquiescence to your request would be detrimental to any future integrative efforts.

BRINGING HOME THE BACON (THE DUNMOW FLITCH TRIALS)

A 'flitch' is an old fashioned word for 'the side of an animal, salted and cured' – what we now refer to as a side of bacon. Dunmow is a village in Essex. Traditionally, a flitch of bacon was given to a couple that could prove they had lived in total marital harmony for at least a year and a day.

Since 1104, trials have taken place periodically to test the validity of claimants. A court is convened with judge and counsel and an opposing counsel (who represent the interests of the flitch donor), together with a jury selected from six maidens and six bachelors. A clerk of the court records the proceedings and an Usher stands in attendance.

Nowadays, the trials take place every four years. A tent is erected in a meadow where a couple desirous of several months' worth of bacon enter and plead their cause. The successful applicants are carried through the village of Dunmow in a carved oak carrying-chair (nowadays a replica) to the centre of the old market place where they renew their marriage vows. Then they return to their domicile – bringing home the bacon. Those unfortunate couples failing to convince the jury of their marital bliss, follow the procession, their faces the pictures of misery, and have to make do with a gammon joint.

This event only takes place when there's a leap year. It started when the Lord of the Manor of Little Dunmow and his wife disguised themselves as peasants and begged the local Augustinian Prior to bless them for never having had a quarrel or a cross word for a year and a day. The Prior was impressed and took pity on them, giving the wretched pair a goodly supply of bacon as a present. Lord Reginald Fitzwalter, for it was he, revealed his true identity and, filled with largesse, declared that the giving of a flitch to happy couples should continue into perpetuity.

Well, it didn't. Henry VIII came along with the dissolution of the monasteries and the flitch trials went out of vogue. People were feeling a bit more cheerful by the 18th century and the practice picked up again.

Then in 1832, Josiah Vine, a retired cheese-monger and, by the sound of it, a professional cheapskate, put the kibosh on it by refusing to let the trials go ahead on his land. A few years later, the flitch trials were transferred from Little Dunmow to Great Dunmow, and there they continue to take place to this day, on an irregular basis.

MARRIAGE ANOMALIES

In future, heirs to the throne will be allowed to marry Roman Catholics, although a Roman Catholic cannot accede to the throne. The anomaly inherent here is that in 1521, the Pope granted Henry VIII the title of '*Fidei Defensor*' (Defender of the Faith) as a reward for a treatise that Henry had written on the scriptures: a diatribe against Luther. Since then, in Britain, kings and queens have called themselves 'Defender of the Faith', oblivious of the fact, it seems, that the faith they are defending is the Roman Catholic faith.

Henry Irving, the first ever-theatrical knight, made his name in a play called *The Bells* at the Lyceum Theatre, London, in 1871. His wife, Florence, was a bit of a snob and thought that acting was rather beneath their dignity. Following his triumphant first night, Irving sat with Florence in a brougham coach as they journeyed home to Fulham. They had reached Hyde Park Corner when Florence said: 'Are you going to make a fool of yourself like this all your life?'

Irving told the driver to stop. Saying nothing more, he got out and sent the coach on its way without him. He never spoke to his wife again.

In the state of New South Wales, Australia, on 31 May 1991, Minnie Munro, aged 101, married Dudley Reid, aged 83, at Point Claire. A search of birth certificates was required to ensure that Minnie wasn't marrying her son.

FIRST-NIGHT NERVES
(AND OTHER SETBACKS)

It's said that a woman's wedding day is something she will never forget. That was certainly true for Princess Maria del Pozzo della Cisterno in 1867. On 30 May, the King of Italy's son, the Duke D'Aosta, was due to tie the knot with Princess Maria. On the morning of the big day her wardrobe mistress hanged herself, the gatekeeper cut his throat and the officer at the head of the wedding parade collapsed with sunstroke. Moreover, the train taking the royal couple to their honeymoon destination was halted when the stationmaster fell to his death underneath it; an aide de camp was crushed by his horse and the Duke's best man shot himself. Even so, the chef is reputed to have asked the princess how she enjoyed the wedding cake.

Archduchess Marie Antoinette travelled in great pomp from Austria to Paris for her pre-arranged marriage. On 16 May 1770, the future king of France, Louis-Auguste, married her. They were 15 and 16 respectively. The Dauphin had eaten like a wolf at the wedding dinner. His father Louis XV cautioned him not to overburden his digestive system on his wedding night. The Dauphin responded: 'Why not? I always sleep better on a full stomach.' Naturally, this raised a few eyebrows.

Later, the newly-weds were escorted to their nuptial chamber with many a suggestive joke being made en route. The entry in the dauphin's diary the following morning simply read, 'Rien.' Nothing. It was not until eight years later, in May 1778, that Louis-Auguste asserted his conjugal rights. During the intervening time, Marie Antoinette gained the reputation for a certain edginess, the reasons for which are not difficult to understand.

King James I joined his friend, Philip Herbert, and his bride in bed on their honeymoon night.

King George III (the 'Mad King') was not allowed to marry his true love, Sarah Lennox, despite the fact that she was the great grand-daughter of King Charles II – her grandmother had been born 'on the wrong side of the blanket'. Was it revenge that prompted George to bring in the Royal Marriages Act of 1772 to bar members of his family from marrying people of whom he disapproved?

When the unpopular Prince Regent became George IV, he found himself obligated in marriage to Caroline of Brunswick. He got so drunk he had to be held up during the ceremony. On his wedding night, he slept like a log and woke up in the fireplace.

A modern legend has developed in Ireland about a man called Albert Muldoon. If the story is correct, it would appear that somewhere in Ireland one day in the 1920s, a village was missing its idiot. Albert had been delegated by some dim groom to be his best man. It is alleged that Mr Muldoon managed to walk up the aisle all right, but at the altar he stood on the left side of the groom instead of the right. The priest addressed his questions to him and Muldoon responded. When it came for the groom to sign the register, it dawned on the priest that an error had occurred. A second ceremony was quickly convened.

Casanova was in the process of marrying one of his younger conquests, a girl called Leonilda. Her mother eagerly offered her services to help with the wedding arrangements. At a later juncture, as the preparations gathered pace, the mother came face to face with her daughter's beau and stared in horror upon recognising him as one of her own former lovers. She fainted but recovered just in time to call off the marriage, preventing Casanova from marrying his own daughter.

Some men are fussy and quote Groucho Marx's remark about his not being willing to join the sort of club that would have him as a member. One high-caste Hindu in particular was heard to opine that he wouldn't want to marry the sort of woman who would sleep with him.

Rudolph Valentino, the famous silent-movie star, impulsively married the American actress Jean Acker in 1919. Immediately, she had second thoughts and locked him out of their honeymoon suite. He stood in the hallway pleading for her to let him in but to no avail. After half an hour, Valentino went silently home. It was one of the shortest marriages on record. This incident tended to tarnish the nickname he had been given by the studios: 'the Latin lover.'

Chapter 10

Same ends – Different means

JUMPING THE BROOM

The time before the American Civil War (1861–5) is known as the antebellum period, a time when marriage between enslaved African-Americans was not legally sanctioned. Slave husbands and wives, without legal recourse, could be separated or sold at their master's will. Couples who lived on separate plantations were allowed to visit only with the consent of their owners.

However, plantation owners encouraged women slaves to have children by promising them their freedom after they'd produced 15 children. This gave the slave owners more manpower. For their own self-respect, enslaved men and women gave themselves a form of loyal declaration. They parodied the old Roma – or Gypsy – wedding traditions that had spread from Eastern Europe into North Africa, and thence to the plantations in America (see Besom weddings, page 93). A wedding party would be arranged on a Saturday night, which culminated in the couple holding hands as they leapt over a broom together, intoning sweet-nothings of love as they did so. Nonetheless, if no offspring were produced, within a year or two, the wife was sold.

MEHNDI PARTIES

In India, a few weeks before the date of her wedding, a bride will hold a 'Mehndi party'. Her family and her female friends help to decorate her body with elaborate designs intended to be a symbolic representation of the outer and the inner sun. In particular, her hands and feet are painted with tumeric (a bright yellow aromatic powder obtained from the rhizome of a plant of the ginger family) and with dye from the henna plant. These intricate designs are difficult to apply, so a long evening party is set aside for the task after which, during the several hours it can take for the 'mehndi' to dry, the bride has to wait patiently, twiddling her thumbs.

PAYING THE RANSOM
(VYKUP NEVESTY)

Before the groom can claim his bride, Russians play a game known as 'Paying the Ransom'. The groom enters and asks to see his beloved. The bride's family leave to fetch her but they return to the room with a strange woman or, preferably, another man in drag. However, this person's face is concealed behind a thick veil. When the groom discovers the deceit, he has to pretend to be distraught and plead for his real love. Then the fun begins. He must cajole the captors of his bride and perform songs and silly dances in an effort to persuade them to release his lady. The family demands a financial ransom for her *(vykup nevesty)*. If the groom is wise he will have come prepared and ensure his pockets are stuffed with coins.

SHOWING THE FACE

Part of a traditional Pakistani wedding is comprised of this variation on paying the ransom. After the marriage, the newly-weds return to the bride's home where her family hold a mirror and a green shawl high in the air above the heads of the couple. The veil that the bride had been wearing previously is ceremoniously removed while the new husband and wife stare lovingly into each other's eyes in the mirror. This distraction is quite deliberate, and the knowing couple play along with it, for while they are staring upwards, moon-eyed, the family has quietly taken the groom's shoes off his feet and hidden them. When the man discovers his loss and begs for his shoes, a ransom is demanded from him for their safe return.

ARRANGED MARRIAGES

Those religious faiths seeking to avoid intermingling with other cultures put the case for arranged marriages most forcefully. In order to maintain the purity of their flocks, devout Catholics, Muslims and, in particular, Hasidic Jews vehemently disapprove of marrying outsiders.

Parents have chosen partners for their children since Biblical times. African, Iranian, Indian and Chinese families frequently arrange marriage contracts for their offspring long before the children are able to express either an opinion or a preference on their own behalf.

Some cultures prefer the men to pay dowries to the bride's family as used to be common in the UK. Others have the woman's family paying the groom. Either way, both families are likely to benefit from the pooling of resources. In developing countries a man may pay with cattle, coin or property. A woman is more likely to pay with gold. In the Middle East, brides traditionally wear their dowry in the form of circlets of gold and coins on their foreheads. If the dowry is substantial, in addition, the lady will wear dazzling earrings and bangles and bracelets of precious jewels (what the sophisticated Westerner today calls 'bling').

Statistics indicate fewer divorces amongst couples that have come together through arranged marriages. The figures are disputed by some who claim the statistics are most likely skewed by religious beliefs.

In Islam, arranged marriages are customary as the best way of finding a fitting partner. However, the consent of the man and/or woman should be obtained. A forced marriage is widely held to be contrary to the teaching of Islam. If a woman disapproves of a potential groom, she has every right to refuse him, and the groom also has the same right. Unfortunately, there remain poverty-stricken places where some parents believe they have the right of life and death over their daughter, and should the young woman refuse to co-operate in an arranged marriage, she runs the risk of being murdered by her own family.

HIEROS GAMOS: SACRED MARRIAGE

Sacred Marriage – or *hieros gamos* – was another symbolic fertility rite, one which tended to culminate in the physical act of sexual intercourse – the ultimate sacrifice to celebrate love and fertility. In the ancient Near East, a high priestess devoted to the worship of Inanna, the Sumerian goddess of love and fertility, would choose a young man to represent Inanna's consort, Dumuzid. During the spring equinox (the New Year) consummation would take place. The Greeks duplicated this overtly symbolic act with a mock wedding between Zeus and Hera – and all in the name of promoting fertility, the prosperity of the community, and the continuation of the cosmos.

The ritual followed a fixed form. First, a procession carried the actors representing the divine characters to the marriage celebration; secondly, there was an exchange of gifts; third, a purification of the pair; fourth, a wedding feast; fifth, a preparation of the wedding chamber and bed; and finally, the nocturnal act of sexual intercourse. The following day a great feast was prepared to celebrate the consummation of the 'marriage'. There is no record as to whether the actors gave encores.

This ritual relating marriage to agriculture, was the mainstay of our ancestors for thousands of years in Mesopotamia, Phoenicia, Canaan, Israel, Greece, and India.

AUSTRALIAN ABORIGINES

Westerners tend to look at the family unit in terms of mother, father, uncles, aunts and cousins and so on. But this concept was foreign to the Australian Aborigines. Their tribes were kept together by their perception of kinship. Fathers, mothers, aunts and uncles were equally responsible to each other and for each other. In times of hardship, two people could become spouses purely through their kinship. One of the few things they sought to avoid, however, was sexual affinity between brother and sister.

Marriages were often arranged shortly after the birth of a girl and the obligations that this involved were closely linked, both materially and spiritually, to the tribal relationship with the land. Such an arrangement was subject to later ratification, mainly through the giving of gifts to the girl's parents. A marriage was accepted as being such when a couple shared their meal around a camp fire and afterwards slept with each other.

It was not unusual for a man to have several wives. In the Tiwi tribe a man could have as many as 29 wives; in the Murngin tribe, two dozen. Many men had 10 to 12. Often a woman would encourage her husband to take on an extra wife in order to help her out with childcare and cooking. A wife would have only one husband at a time, although she was quick to marry again should her husband die or the marriage break up.

PERUVIAN TRADITION

There is a quaint custom in Peru that gives a chance of romantic success to singletons attending a wedding. Between the layers of wedding cake, small amulets and trinkets are hidden and tied to ribbons. As soon as the bride and groom have cut the first slice, each of the bridesmaids and attendant women grab a ribbon and pull. Just one of these ribbons has an imitation wedding ring attached to the end. The women fervently hope that whoever selects the ring is the next one to marry.

PAPUA NEW GUINEA – TRIBAL WEDDINGS

Eight hundred languages are spoken in Papua New Guinea, which gives some idea of the number of small tribes there. Traditional tribal marriages are commercial transactions; the groom's family negotiates a price with the family of the prospective bride from another tribe.

The bride's price is measured in pigs, shells and, nowadays, hard cash – albeit in small amounts. Sometimes, several suitors will plight their troth for the same woman, particularly if she is the daughter of a tribal chief. In such cases, she can command a high price, perhaps as many as 30 pigs. In most cases, however, four or five pigs will seal the deal. A couple of these swine will be fattened in anticipation of the wedding feast.

On the big day, bare-breasted women will paint themselves according to the style of their clan – hands, arms, backs and faces with streaks of yellow, red and blue. It is the tradition for the couple and all guests to wear grass skirts. The men paint themselves in their ceremonial colours and wear a breastplate of coloured seashells. Brightly coloured feathers and dead birds are woven into their hair.

The men form a line and face the women. They chant and sing and dance. The couple getting hitched stand between the two lines and are encouraged to hold hands while a carnival atmosphere develops. The pigs are led into the circle, from which the bride's mother makes her selection for the feast. The slaughtered pigs are roasted on banana leaves and the celebrations begin. The marriage is complete.

PYGMY MARRIAGES

The average height of the Bambuti Pygmies (aka Mbuti tribe) of the Congo region is less than 4 ft 6 in. Their blood group is unique in that part of Africa, emphasising the isolation of a people whose presence was first recorded by the Egyptians 4,500 years ago. The thick, tropical Ituri Rainforest is an uneasy place to make a living, but the Pygmies nomadic lifestyle has not prevented them from breeding. Pygmy babies are, proportionally, the biggest babies in the world. They are, typically, one-tenth of the body weight of their mother. Pygmies consider a woman's breasts to be specifically for feeding and they are never used for sexual stimulation.

Bride price (also known as 'bride wealth' and 'bride token'), common in African countries, is an amount of wealth or property paid by a groom's family to the parents of the potential bride. Amongst the Pygmies, though, it is rarely enforced.

Pygmy marriages are based on a reciprocal agreement whereby an allied family with an eligible sister or brother in one clan is exchanged for a brother or sister in another. This is a loose arrangement and the exchange may not be completed until the boy or girl is sufficiently mature.

There is little in the way of a formal ceremony. Once an

exchange has been agreed, the groom will leave the tribe and go away on a solitary odyssey. He will not return until he has killed a sufficiently valuable offering such as an antelope. He presents his prize to the intended bride's parents, as proof of his prowess. Pygmies follow a patrilineal descent system, and after the feast of antelope, the bride will return with the hunter to his family home. Few Pygmies are polygynous (that is, a man having more than one wife, the commonest form of polygamy).

TRADITIONAL CHINESE WEDDINGS

When Chinese ladies make up their minds to get hitched, the likelihood is they will be ordering their wedding dresses in red, the colour that denotes happiness in China. To add contrast, a touch of white here and there is acceptable. Blue, black or grey are unthinkable. It follows then that more than half of the world's population prefer their marriages to be couched in red – including the candles.

A little background history might help to understand the Chinese attitude to weddings…

During the thousand years when the empires of ancient Greece and Rome were rising and falling, on the other side of the then known world in the unconquered East of Asia, a totally different culture was developing.

In what we now call China, there was a great deal of territorial disagreement. Historians refer to those years as the Warring States period. The genesis of the Chinese wedding ceremony began then, but it was complicated, and varied from village to village. As unification of the country grew, so did the simplification of marriage.

Four basic objectives remain that can be reconciled with Western concepts.

1. Merging of two families for mutual interest.
2. Progeny to ensure legitimate inheritance.
3. Respect to parents and forefathers.
4. Financial prosperity.

As well as all this, a desirable but not essential outcome is the bride's immersion into the bosom of her husband's family. The process of a marriage proposal between the two parties is still entrusted to a professional matchmaker, although the parents of the prospective couple take ultimate responsibility for the match.

If all goes well, the date and hour of the girl's birth is registered and this testament is placed on the ancestral altar for three days. If nobody has second thoughts and everyone continues to be in agreement, an astrologer is brought in to check that the young man and the young woman have compatible horoscopes.

When the astrologer agrees that the signs are auspicious, the procedure carries forward to the actual proposal. In the enforced absence of the prospective bride and groom, both sides of the family meet and exchange ideas. Again, with astrological guidance, if everything is satisfactory, dates are agreed, and the nature of betrothal presents settled on. The groom's father presents items of food and, in particular, tea. Such betrothal gifts are collectively known as cha-li – 'tea presents'. The woman's family responds with clothing. They also undertake to distribute the bridal cakes that have been donated by the groom's family.

After the betrothal has been satisfactorily completed, the prospective wedding is deemed binding. At this stage, the bride and groom have probably not yet met. Indeed, the bride and groom might still be children. Betrothal and the exchange of gifts could continue for years until the pair become mature enough to marry.

As the wedding day approaches, the girl withdraws into seclusion, and during her isolation she will sing laments about her imminent separation from her family. Meanwhile, astrologers advise the groom of the best hour of day to install the bridal bed, which is brought in and made up accordingly. Babies are invited and encouraged to crawl all over it. The bed is scattered with seeds – lotus, pomegranate, dates and other fruit – to bring fertility to the marriage bed.

On the morning of the wedding, the bride lights dragon and phoenix candles to frighten away the evil spirits. Sitting in close proximity to the candles as a sort of protective cover, she slips into her brand new underclothes. The ritual then demands that she undergo the hair dressing ritual. The hairdresser is a 'good luck woman' and as she shapes the bride's hair into the style deemed correct for a married woman, she delivers a mantra of 'dos and don'ts' to the bride.

After this, the bride's costume is completed with red shoes and a red silk veil and at the appointed time, she is carried to the main event. She bows to her parents and awaits the arrival of the groom with his party.

Meanwhile, the groom has been dressed in a long gown with a red silk sash and a pair of red shoes. On his head his father places a cap decorated with cypress leaves. At last, the groom is ready to go and meet his bride. He bows, first to the altar of his ancestors and second to his parents, before climbing into a sedan chair and leading the procession to the bride's house where he is to take possession of her. A great rigmarole accompanies him – firecrackers, drums and gongs. Dancers and musicians whirl around where they sit enthroned.

On arrival, he is made to 'pay his fee' – money in red envelopes – before being admitted. Inside the house, the bride's parents have prepared a feast of eggs and noodles and other delicacies. Once he has been accepted and fed at the table of her parents, the bride's feet are bound together and she is lifted by her hairdresser, 'the good-luck woman', and carried to the sedan chair. How reminiscent of our primal ancestor dragging the reluctant woman to his cave. And how universal is the human fear of the dark.

Firecrackers are set off to frighten evil spirits. To conceal unlucky sights from the eyes of the bride, she sits in the sedan chair behind thick curtains. She is shielded from any cats, graves or widows that may have been lining the route. Seeds, rice and beans, symbols of fertility, are strewn in her path.

A red carpet lies before the house of the groom so that the bride's feet will not touch the dirty earth. In some provinces of China, she might be required to step over a red stove or a saddle in order to gain entrance to the house. Apparently, the Chinese words for 'saddle' and 'peace' sound similar (*ngan*). Through such verbal misunderstandings, traditions are born.

Once the fly is in the spider's web, the groom can at last raise his bride's red veil and see for himself what she looks like. The marriage ceremony itself is short and to the point. The couple stands before the family altar where they pay obeisance to the God of the Kitchen, Tsao-Chun. The groom's parents drink tea in which two lotus seeds have been added.

After the wedding dinner, the bride and groom are led to their nuptial chamber where they drink wine laced with honey. The following morning the young bride makes breakfast for her parents-in-law. With their approval, she returns to her boudoir. This Chinese honeymoon will last for three days, open to public inspection and encouraging banter.

(There are about three billion Chinese in the world, so whatever they get up to in the bridal chamber, it evidently works well. The tried and tested formula is practised to this day, but the government of China encourages families to limit themselves to one child only. There is a system of increasingly punitive tax for every child after the firstborn.)

After three days, the newly-weds return to the bride's family home to pay their respects. The bride is formally received as a guest.

CONTEMPORARY CHINESE WEDDINGS

Chinese New Year varies according to the placement of the stars in the zodiac. For example, in 2013 it started on 10 February – being the year of the snake; in 2014 it started on 31 January – the year of the horse; and in 2015 it starts on 19 February – the year of the goat or lamb.

Almanacs are issued at the beginning of each Chinese New Year predicting which days will be auspicious in conjunction with the planets. Professional astrologers (or feng shui experts) are given the birth dates of possible future brides and grooms, and after the almanacs have been studied, the families will be told the most auspicious astrological influences available for their offspring. It goes without saying that the one period to avoid is the Hungry Ghost Festival, when the gates of hell are unlocked for a fortnight and the spirits wander round their old haunts for a while.

In modern China, a bride might wear up to three dresses for her wedding day. First, there is the traditional red *qipao* or *cheongsam*. Next, comes a white flouncy ball gown influenced by American marriages. Finally, after the reception, she will probably change into a cocktail dress in colours of her own choosing.

Chinese tea ceremony

At Chinese weddings, tea is drunk in preference to champagne because tea is the national drink of China. Into the tea are put two red dates and some lotus seeds. The symbolism stems from the homophones for these words in Chinese (same sound but different meanings). 'Lotus' sounds like 'year', 'seed' sounds like 'baby', and 'date' like 'speedy'. Words that look difficult to pronounce to Western ears are child's play to those from East Asia. Putting these ingredients together encourages the spirits to create an early pregnancy. The tea is mixed with honey to promote sweetness between the couple and on their saucers they will find lucky red envelopes (*lai see*) stuffed with money placed there surreptitiously by the father of the bride.

SPARTAN MARRIAGES

Spartans (from the city-state of Sparta) were a particularly odd group whose peccadilloes seem strange to us today and, to be fair, seemed pretty odd to their contemporaneous Greeks.

The ordinary Greeks from Athens followed the widespread marriage ritual already described on page 138. On the eve of her wedding, the Spartan girl took a bath from a sacred spring and swore fealty to the goddess of agriculture, Demeter. The following day, as dusk fell, the bride joined a procession to the home of the groom, her route being lit by outriders with torches.

Until the day of the wedding, neither bride nor groom would have seen each other's faces, and right up until the last minute the bride wore an opaque veil.

In Aphrodisias, the women followed the curious custom of becoming prostitutes in the Temple of Aphrodite before they were married. Going on the game for them meant they could accumulate a large sum of money to donate to the goddess Artemis, as well as assimilating some practical expertise (an extreme example of 'the bottom drawer'?). Any women who protested against this behaviour had their heads shaved as a forfeit.

Spartan women had their hair cut short as a matter of fashion. And they dressed as men. As they grew into nubile women, they allowed themselves to be kidnapped by men. These women could not look forward to a special wedding day and had to make do with a brief, private ceremony.

Naturally, this sort of treatment gave Spartan women a hard edge. For example, after she had polished her son's shield, a mother would hand it back to him before he went off to battle, saying, 'Here's your clean shield, son. Go out and fight. Come back with your shield... Or on it.'

The night before a Spartan groom got married, his comrades in arms gave him a feast. At the conclusion of the evening, the groom reassured his pals that whatever befell him, they would always be first in his affections and he would stick by them to the end.

According to the historian Plutarch, come the wedding night, the groom spent a short time with his wife on the marriage bed before slipping back into his usual quarters to sleep with his old male buddies. It was for behaviour like this that Spartan men are given the credit for being the originators of the stag party of today.

Even after marriage, the bride was not allowed to live in the same house as her husband. A Spartan man's first duty was to his military unit. He couldn't move in with his wife until he was 30, assuming he survived that long.

ISLAMIC MARRIAGES

The Qur'an teaches those of the Muslim faith that if they are to satisfy their sexual desires then they should marry. According to a saying of Muhammad, marriage is regarded as being half of one's faith and should be undertaken regardless of wealth or poverty. Money has to be paid to a prospective wife by a Muslim man before marriage. This money is known as the *mahr* (dowry or bride gift) and it is given to her so that when she becomes a wife, she cannot claim to be poverty stricken: when a husband becomes part of her life, she will be starting off with her own nest egg.

A Muslim wedding is known as a *nikah*. The technicalities of Islamic marriages are not dissimilar to the Roman marriage, although during the ceremony, the bride says absolutely nothing. Muslims come from a wide range of cultures and it would be a mistake to say all Islamic weddings are similar. The essence of a Muslim wedding is within the actual Islamic religious ceremony. A registry office service wouldn't, in all honesty, cut the mustard. However, a civil licence may still be necessary if marrying in a mosque.

There is a burgeoning of mosques in England but, oddly, not all of them have been registered with the authorities as places of worship. Many are mere meeting places for Islamists. It follows that a wedding in a mosque, though satisfactory from the point of view of the Islamic clerics and the mosque leaders, is not necessarily legal in the eyes of UK law, and another civil ceremony may have to take place in order to register for any benefits in the UK to which a married couple might be entitled.

GIPSY & ROMANY WEDDINGS

Gypsies were travellers hailing from India. They called themselves Roma or Romany, meaning a tribe or group of people sharing the same physical characteristics, namely dark hair and dark skin. Nowadays, the Roma people are gradually starting to settle. The Roma language is derived from Sanskrit, the primary language of Hinduism. 'Gypsy' is a 16th-century word and is a corruption of *gipscyan* meaning Egyptian. At that time, Gypsies were mistakenly believed to have originated in North Africa.

In England intermarriage was outlawed between Gypsies and the settled population. If a non-Gypsy woman married a Gypsy man, she had to conform to the conventions of Gypsy society.

Gypsy marriages can be achieved by resorting to one of these three methods:

1. Abduction
2. Purchase
3. Mutual consent

In Gypsy culture, a girl can marry soon after the age of 13 and a boy on reaching puberty. According to Roma laws, it is up to the boy's parents to find a suitable girl for their son to marry. If a girl rejects a proposal, the boy's family suffers a great loss of face. If she accepts, there follows protracted wrangling over the *darro* (dowry).

Once the *darro* is agreed, there is a special celebration to announce the wedding. This is called the *pliashka*. The prospective groom's father places a necklace of gold coins around the bride-to-be's neck. A glass of wine is shared to signify mutual acceptance.

Bread and salt are key objects at the wedding ceremony. The expression 'Let us take bread and salt' is used by Gypsies in much the same way as the rest of us say, 'Let us tie the knot'.

The bride brings bread, salt and a jug of water to the ceremony. Shallow incisions are made in the groom's right wrist and the bride's left wrist. The cut wrists are held together for the bloods to mingle. The couple's wrists are bound together with a silk cord which has three knots tied in it: a knot for fertility, a knot for constancy, and a knot for long life.

The Elder takes a piece of bread and smears it with the blood of the couple. The bride and groom are each handed a piece of the blooded bread, which they must eat. The remains of the bread is crumbled and thrown over them. The silk cord that binds their wrists is then cut, with half being given to the husband and half to the wife. They must safeguard these ties for two years. If they decide to divorce, the two halves of cord are brought together and ritually burnt by the Elder before witnesses.

Once the marriage ceremony is over, the new wife is presented with a *dilko* – a married woman's headscarf – by her mother-in-law. Henceforth, she must never be seen in public without it.

HINDU MARRIAGES

Hinduism is the oldest surviving religion in the world. The majority of Hindus live in India and conduct their weddings in the ancient language of Sanskrit. The ceremonies are colourful affairs and the conviviality goes on for days, although there are regional variations. Since 1955, when the Hindu Marriage Act was passed in India, all Hindus of any sect, creed or caste can intermarry. This includes Buddhists, Jains and Sikhs.

The ritual starts with the pre-wedding declaration of intent. It ends eventually with the post-wedding ceremonies when the bride is welcomed to her new home and a yellow woollen bracelet (*kautu-kasutra*) is tied around the wrist of the betrothed girl by her mother.

The marriage ceremony sometimes takes place under a marriage pavilion (pandal). In the same way that carrying aloft a torch was symbolic in the Roman tradition, so the Sacred Fire (the deity Agni) is a key witness to a Hindu marriage. The bride and groom must circle the Sacred Fire seven times to seal the deal. A swing (*dola*) is set up under the pandal on which the couple seat themselves after the ceremony. The swing symbolises the union between earth and sky.

JAIN MARRIAGES

The word 'Jain' comes from the word 'Jina', which means a conqueror and comes from the root 'Ji' (to conquer). It means conquering the passions. In the Jain religion, with its emphasis on non-violence, a public proclamation has to be made by the groom and bride to declare their intention of living together.

At the bride's house, a priest sets the date for the time of the wedding. The priest goes to the groom's house and a ritual known as a *puja* is enacted. For Hindus, of which Jain is a sect, there are several kinds of pujas, often astrological in their origin, all showing reverence to the Almighty God. Specific mantras are chanted for marriage.

The jewelled headpiece known as a tikka or *jhoomar* is a mandatory part of the bride's ornament on the day of her marriage. One of the bride's male relatives applies a mark to the forehead of the groom and gifts are given to him – money, clothes, gold or tokens. Then the priest reads out the date of the wedding. The groom gives the bride's closest male relative a coconut and the Hindu ritual of lighting the sacred flame (*aarti*) is now enacted. The flames are lit from wicks soaked in purified butter known as *ghee*. These are offered up to the deities as married women from the bride's family sing traditional *aarti* songs of praise.

The father of the bride performs Kanyadaan ritual. He places one rupee and 25 paise, and some rice, in his daughter's right palm and hands her to the bridegroom. While chanting mantras, the priest pours holy water on the hands of the couple. This is followed by the *granthi bandhan*, in which a married woman ties the knot between the bride's sari and the groom's shawl.

After this, the couple takes the seven vows (*saat phere*), the most important ritual in the Jain wedding. They start by forming a circle with their families round the fire. In the first round, the newly-weds pray to God to let them walk together so that they will have an abundance of food. In the second round, they pray to God for health, both spiritual and physical. In the third round, they pray for wealth. In the fourth, they pray that their love will grow for each other and for their respective families; in the fifth, for all God's children to be healthy, wealthy and wise; in the sixth, for a peaceful life together; and in the seventh round, that their mutual understanding and loyalty will last for a lifetime.

Following the completion of the vows, the bride is regarded as *Vamangi*, and she becomes her husband's 'better half'. The couple exchange garlands. Finally, the ritual is completed with *Shantipath* and *Visarjan* (a mantra praying for peace and harmony followed by the blessing of Ganesh statues in holy water).

Once the wedding rituals are over, the elders come forward to bless the newly-weds for their forthcoming marital life. This is known as the *Ashirvada* ceremony.

JEWISH WEDDINGS

Practising Jews, in particular, Hasidic Jews, take a strict line on marrying outside the Faith. The Gentile who would be a groom or a bride has to conform by converting to Judaism, otherwise the man or woman who marries a Gentile risks becoming a lost sheep. On top of this, a professional matchmaker arranges most Jewish marriages. Strict self-policing such as this helped exempt Jewish weddings from the provisions of the Marriage Act of 1753 (see Lord Hardwicke, page 149).

In the Talmud (the ultimate authority on Jewish behaviour) it is expressly written: 'He who does not marry is like a murderer and he violates the image of God.' Thus, as in most other religions, marriage has become the most significant festival in domestic life.

It is customary for the groom and the bride not to see each other for one week preceding the wedding. As a consequence, by the time the day arrives they are both champing at the bit.

The nine elements of a Jewish wedding are as follows:

The Ketubah (that which is written): Unless the rights of the intended bride are protected, the marriage cannot go ahead, so first of all, the groom (chatan) reads the marriage contract – the ketubah. The rabbi will reaffirm the chatan's commitment towards the end of the ceremony.

The Bedeken (the veiling ceremony): After the ketubah is signed, the chatan approaches the bride (kallah) and lifts her thick veil. This is to reassure everybody that he is marrying the woman of his choice. The chatan does not want to make the same mistake as his ancestor, Jacob, who failed to notice, until it was too late, that he had married Leah instead of her sister, Rachel.

The Huppah, or Chuppah – (Jewish wedding canopy with four open sides): This is a square cloth, about 5 by 6 ft, made of cotton or silk and supported by four poles. Standing under the huppah is symbolic of the couple standing together in their new home. The huppah is often kept afterwards as a wall covering or a shawl. Canopies such as these are not unique to Jewish weddings. They were used in medieval English ceremonies, and to this day are found in Hindu and Jain weddings. It is said that if the chatan (groom) puts his foot on that of the kallah (bride), he will rule the roost. If she manages to get her foot on his foot first, then she will wear the pants. Underneath the huppah, the chatan and his kallah make seven tight circuits, representing the seven days of creation. The kallah then stops on the right-hand side of the chatan.

The Kudushin (betrothal blessing): The rabbi recites a blessing of betrothal and the couple drinks from the same goblet of wine. The chatan says: 'With this ring you are now consecrated to me according to the Law of Moses and Israel.' He places the wedding ring on the index finger of his bride's right hand. According to the Torah this gift – the ring – must be plain and unadorned. The act of marriage has now taken place.

The Nissuin (marriage): The rabbi reads the ketubah again, with a translation so there is no danger of misinterpretation.

Sheva Brachot (the seven blessings): Over a second glass of wine, the seven blessings are recited.

Mazel tov (good fortune): After the blessings the married couple drain the wine and the glass is placed on the floor. The chatan crushes it with the heel of his shoe. This is a reminder of the sadness felt at the destruction of the Temple in Jerusalem and as a reminder of Israel's sorrows. Jewish humourists have said that this moment is the last time a married man gets to put his foot down. As the glass is smashed, the guests will shout, 'Mazel tov!'

The Yichud (the bridal suite): The newly-weds are escorted to a private room where they will do whatever takes their fancy for a short while. Sephardim Jews, made of sterner stuff, miss out this exciting stage of the ceremony, and go straight through to the festive Memal.

The Seudah (the festive meal): Rather like any wedding feast of any denomination, there is a lot of eating and drinking, ribaldry and laughter.

Among the ancient Hebrews there was a distinction between a promise and a betrothal. A promise might mean an engagement without a definite follow-through. There could be a number of engagements, each broken off. The betrothal was a binding commitment. The promise may be set aside but a betrothal was a covenant.

In Biblical times, the groom would dress as closely to his

idea of a king as he could afford, crown and all. The bride obeyed the words of David: 'Our daughters may be as corner stones, polished after the similitude of a palace.' Accordingly, her face would be scrubbed until her complexion was as lustrous as marble. Her hair would be glossy and bedecked with gold, pearls and jewels that had been passed down to her through the generations. A thick veil concealed her face.

The Lubavitch Hasidic sect takes its Orthodox Judaism very seriously. Their weddings demand that the groom has no knots anywhere about his person. Therefore, before starting the process of marriage, he must remove his tie and untie his shoelaces and so on. Apparently, this is to start him on the right road where no knotty marital problems will fall across his path.

In the Middle Ages a wedding dance called the *mitzvah* materialised. Because of the segregation of the sexes, the groom danced with other men and the bride with ladies. The rules relaxed with time. By wearing gloves or by holding a piece of cloth between their bodies, the bride was allowed to dance with men of the family. Dancing with the bride is considered an act of devotion and the officiating rabbi is only too pleased to oblige.

LEBANESE WEDDINGS

Lebanese weddings start with shouting and banging outside the house of the groom. When the husband-to-be comes out of the door, the rowdiness is replaced with music and singing, with professional dancers joining in. This is known as the *zaffe*. The groom's family and friends escort him to collect the bride from her home. They are then sent off to the ceremony in a shower of flower petals.

MALAYSIAN WEDDINGS

Intricately decorated eggs are distributed as symbols of fertility in a Malaysian wedding tradition. To make a wedding legal in Malaysia a religious solemnisation known as the *Nikah* (marriage) rites has to be performed on the night before the wedding ceremony takes place. The *pelamin* (bridal couch) is the centrepiece for the couple on their big day. The bride and groom take their places on it side by side during the *bersanding* (joining together). During the ceremony, friends of the bride and groom apply a yellow oil extracted from henna leaves to the fingertips of the couple.

MAORI MARRIAGE

Kia ora! (Hello there)

Until the 20th century, the Maori married according to their own traditions. For example, in 1887 there were only 13 marriages between Maori conducted under colonial legislation, that is to say, English common law. In those days, the Maori would have been puzzled had their young people not had sex whenever they could. Indeed, youngsters were expected to have several partners before settling down to start a family of their own. A young man was considered to be serious in his attentions only when he started to shower the object of his heart's desire with gifts such as greenstone ornaments, flax coats, bird spears, whalebone clubs and other useful things for providing food on the table.

Because of their fearsome appearance in rugby matches, Maori people have the reputation for being warlike but there is another side to their nature that shows them to be more like pussycats. In the era before colonial rule, the concept of marriage as Westerners think of it was unknown to the

Maori. They were romantics and believed in true love as typified in the oft-repeated love story of their ancestors, Princess Hinemoa and Tutanekai.

Tutanekai, the Romeo of this story, lived on Mokoia Island in the centre of Rotorua lake. He was the adopted son of a good family, but not good enough for a princess, or so her family believed. (Rotorua is in the centre of the North Island of New Zealand, where the earth's crust is thin and hot water bubbles to the surface, shooting geysers high into the air and creating thermal mud pools. Your chronicler has bathed in the hot mud pools of Rotorua, which are said to be most beneficial to one's health.)

Anyway, back to the love story. Princess Hinemoa was grounded by her parents and kept in her home village of Owhata on the shores of the lake. She pined for the boy she had met on Mokoia Island. When the wind was blowing in the right direction she could hear Tutanekai playing a plaintive tune on his flute. She was stopped from going to him and her family beached the canoes.

After many days of unrequited agony, Hinemoa lashed together several gourds to make a raft. That night, guided by the flute, she paddled to Mokoia Island where she collapsed with exhaustion. She was awakened by a servant filling a gourd with water. On learning that this servant worked for Tutaneki's father, she smashed the gourd. He plucked another gourd from a calabash tree and tried to fill that instead but she smashed that as well. The servant ran back and relayed what had happened.

Tutaneki went to investigate. He carried a club and was on the point of killing the intruder when she turned and announced herself. Astonished that she had been brave enough to run away from home, he took her back to his little hut and from that moment they lived as man and wife and never separated again.

The parents of the couple went to search for them. When they looked into the hut they saw four feet instead of two, and so they acquiesced and the lovers were left in peace.

These days, during a simple Maori wedding ceremony, the highpoint is when Tutaneki's song is sung. Here is an English translation:

Verse
They are stirred
The waters of Lake Rotorua
Cross over to me girl
For now they are calm.

Chorus
Oh girl
Return to me
Or else I will die
Because of my love for you.

Verse
I have written my letter
I have sent you my ring
So that your people can see
That I am troubled.

Chorus
Oh girl
Return to me
Or else I will die
Because of my love for you.

There's a distinct possibility that this song loses something in translation.

An important part of the modern ceremony seems to consist of the 'rubbing of noses' (the *hongi*), a greeting that appears to be in the same tradition as that practised by the Inuit in the opposite hemisphere.

QUAKER WEDDINGS

Quakers are officially known as the Religious Society of Friends. The founder of the organisation was George Fox who, in 1669, married Margaret Fell without the benefit of clergy, eliciting accusations that they were living in sin. There are more than 350,000 Quakers in the world and it is understood that many of them consider themselves as part of a universal religion steeped in Christian tradition. They believe that Man has a fundamental direct link with his Maker, and that there is no need for intermediaries such as the Church or ordained priests. Regular meetings are held for contemplation and discussion, and whatever subject is under discussion, the group seeks a consensus of unity.

At a Meeting of Friends, a couple may declare their wish to marry. A 'clearness committee' is then set up to discuss their proposal and to decide upon its suitability.

In European countries, same-sex marriages are considered as being on equal terms to heterosexual unions. If there are no obvious impediments, the couple will be helped by the Friends to obtain the necessary legal documents and a Quaker wedding certificate. A notice of 'Intention to Marry' is mailed to the local superintendent registrar.

A special Meeting is convened at the Friends Meeting House, where the congregation sits with the couple in silent contemplation for a while. It is necessary for a qualified registrar to be present.

At length, the couple will announce their 'declarations' to God, witnessed by the Friends who are listening, for they believe that to marry 'is God's ordinance and not man's.... It is the Lord's work, and we are His witnesses.' The registrar draws up the certificate and all those present sign as witnesses. The couple walks away as husband and wife.

RUSSIAN WEDDINGS

Russian wedding festivities can spread over two or three days, the actual ceremony being only a small part of the celebration. The bride and groom arrive separately and are kept apart until they are called. Once in the registration hall, they are hailed by the registrar and dusted with bread and salt. The couple are led to the place where the actual rites will be read. Here they stand on a special carpet and the official reads a short speech before asking the bride and groom if they 'do'. Once they've said yes, the pair exchange rings and sign the register. The witnesses append their signatures too, after which the newly-weds are officially man and wife. A capacity for both vodka and non-stop dancing is required.

SIKH MARRIAGES

The Sikh marriage ceremony is known also as *Anand Karaj*, meaning 'blissful union'. Anand Karaj consists of the couple revolving around *Sri Guru Granth Sahib* (the holy book of the Sikh religion, which contains the hymns of Sikh gurus) four times while the marriage hymns are recited. Revolving signifies that the *Guru* scripture is the centre of the couple's life and the acknowledgement of the soul crossing this world to be one with God.

In Sikhism, when a girl attains maturity, it is the duty of her parents to find a suitable match for her, preferably with another Sikh. Sikh marriages are usually arranged: this means a mutual agreement between the man and the woman on the one part, and his and her parents on the other (see Arranged marriages, page 214).

By the tenets of Sikh religion, marriage is regarded as a sacred bond that cannot be undone. Divorce can only be obtained under civil law. The marriage ceremony is conducted in a *gurdwara* (place of worship) or at the bride's home or any other suitable place where *Guru Granth Sahib* scripture is duly installed. A priest or any Sikh (man or woman) may conduct the ceremony.

When the vows of the couple have been honoured, they are asked to bow together before the *Guru Granth Sahib*. The bride's father places one end of a saffron-coloured scarf in the groom's hand, passing it over the shoulder and placing the other end in the bride's hand. Thus joined, the two will take the vows. This is followed by a short hymn.

The musicians sing the same verse again while the couple slowly encircles *Guru Granth Sahib*. The groom leads in a clockwise direction and the bride, holding the scarf, follows as nearly as possible in step. The four verses of the *Lavan* (hymn) explain the four stages of love and married life. The first *Lavan* emphasises the performance of duty to the family and the community. The second signifies the stage of yearning and love for each other; the third the stage of detachment; and the final *Lavan* signifies the mature stage of harmony and union in married life during which human love blends into the love for God.

Certain rituals, common in other religions, are forbidden in Sikhism, including the tying of headbands, any pretence at sulkiness or false naivety, the drinking of alcohol and the burning of so-called sacred fires.

ZULU WEDDINGS

Where a dowry is deemed necessary in Western societies, it is customary for the bride's family to supply it. In South Africa it is usually the other way round. The man pays the equivalent of a dowry to the prospective bride's family as proof of his capability to support a wife. This is known as 'The bride price' or *lobolo/lobola.* A cash transaction is sometimes made, but traditionally, *lobolo* is paid in the form of cattle.

If the bride and groom come from separate tribes with different customs, the bride follows the culture of the groom. Accordingly, the groom calls a gathering of both families to his home. After a date has been agreed, wedding preparations begin in earnest. The bride and her family prepare her 'dowry box' putting together such items as pots and pans, blankets and furniture, and other items of domesticity suitable to furnish her future home.

In the Zulu religion, it is believed that their ancestral spirits act as mediators between the temporal life and Umvelinqangi (God's holy messenger). Consequently, the chief of the bride's clan will make a sacrifice – usually a cow – to his ancestors to forewarn them that she is leaving the clan. This ceremony is known as *umncamo.* The groom's family will slaughter a goat or a cow to prove that there is food available for the new member of the clan and to welcome the newcomer. This is called the ritual of *indlakudla.*

Early on the morning of the wedding day, the bride will be brought from her *kraal* (homestead) by her father and pointed in the direction of the groom's home with the instruction that she is not to look back. When she arrives, the groom's family turns away from her, pretending not to notice her unheralded entrance. The bride goes straight to the woman's side of the home and takes her place in the kitchen. There she is welcomed with great élan and the celebrations begin. She is feted and shown the room she will share with her husband. A feast follows with much dancing and singing.

In a Zulu marriage, should the husband die within the first few years, a brother must marry the woman on behalf of his dead sibling, and must try his best to beget children.

Chapter 11

The last word in weddings

WEDDING LINES

Soothsayers and palmists claim that there is one (sometimes several) short line below the base of the little finger, just above the heart line. If this is strong and clear, the palmist will predict marriage. More than one line indicates more than one marriage. It is hard to imagine what a palmist would make of the palm-prints of Elizabeth Taylor or Zsa Zsa Gabor – they both married eight times.

Here are some of the wry conclusions they drew from their first-hand experience of marital disunion, starting with Zsa Zsa (b. 1917), who is alleged to have said: 'I am a marvellous housekeeper. Every time I leave a man, I keep his house.' She had many other things to say on the subject…

'A man is incomplete until he marries. Then he's finished.'
'You never really know a man until you've divorced him.'
'I know nothing about sex because I was always married.'
'How many husbands have I had? You mean, apart from my own?'
'Conrad Hilton was very generous to me in the divorce settlement. He gave me 5,000 Gideon Bibles.'
'I never hated a man enough to give him the diamonds back.'
'Husbands are like fires. They go out when unattended.'
'I want a man who is kind and understanding. Is that too much to ask of a millionaire?'

Elizabeth Taylor, actress (1932–2011), commented:

> 'I suppose when they reach a certain age, some men are afraid to grow up. It seems the older the men get, the younger their new wives get.'

Mae West (1893–1980), writer/actress, known for her double-entendres, also had a few things to say on the subject:

> 'Marriage is a great institution, but I'm not ready for an institution.'
> 'Men are my hobby. If I ever got married I'd have to give it up.'
> 'Opportunity knocks for every man, but you have to give a woman a ring.'
> 'Too much of a good thing can be wonderful.'
> 'Some women pick men to marry. Others pick them to pieces.'
> 'Brains are an asset to the woman in love who is smart enough to hide them.'
> 'He who hesitates is last.'
> 'Don't keep a man guessing too long. He's sure to find the answer somewhere else.'
> 'Save a boyfriend for a rainy day – and another, in case it doesn't.'
> 'Getting married is like trading in the adoration of many for the sarcasm of one.'

There have been many other commentators on the institution of marriage:

Mrs Patrick Campbell (1865–1940), actress: 'Wedlock: the deep, deep peace of the double bed after the hurly-burly of the chaise longue.'

Aristotle (384–322 BC): 'Love is composed of a single soul inhabiting two bodies.'

Quentin Crisp (1908–99), raconteur: 'Why get married? For human beings, marriage is such an unnatural state. If you want monogamy, it has been said, you should marry a swan.'

Ingrid Bergman (1915–82), actress: 'A kiss is a lovely trick designed by nature to stop speech when words become superfluous.'

H Jackson Brown, Jr. (b. 1940), author: 'Sometimes the heart sees what is invisible to the eye.'

Oscar Wilde (1854–1900), poet: 'To love oneself is the beginning of a lifelong romance.' And: 'Bigamy is having one husband or wife too many. Monogamy is the same.'

Lady (Nancy) Astor (1879–1964), first woman MP to take her seat in Parliament: 'I married beneath me. All women do.'

Francis Bacon (1561–1626), statesman: 'Wives are young men's mistresses; companions for middle age, and old men's nurses.'

Alan King (1927–2004), comedian: 'Marriage is nature's way of keeping people from fighting with strangers.'

Erich Fromm (1900–80), psychologist: 'Immature love says, "I love you because I need you." Mature love says, "I need you because I love you".'

Max Kauffman (b.1940), artist: 'I never knew what real happiness was until I got married. And by then it was too late.'

That old fellow, Anon.: 'Marriage means commitment. Of course, so does insanity.'

Another gem attributed to **Anon.**: 'Marriage is not a word – it is a sentence.'

Voltaire (1694–1778), philosopher: 'God created sex. Priests created marriage.'

Marilyn Monroe (1926–62), actress: 'Before marriage, a girl has to make love to a man to hold him. After marriage, she has to hold him to make love to him.'

Jerry Hall (b.1956), model: 'My mother said it was simple to keep a man: you must be a maid in the living room, a cook in the kitchen and a whore in the bedroom. I said I'd hire the other two and take care of the bedroom bit.'

Lyndon B Johnson (1908–73), President of USA: 'I have learned that only two things are necessary to keep one's wife happy. First, let her think she's having her own way. And second, let her have it.'

James A Baldwin (1924–87), writer: 'Love does not begin and end the way we seem to think it does. Love is a battle, love is a war; love is a growing up.'

Leo J Burke (1911–80), teacher: 'The husband who doesn't tell his wife everything probably reasons that what she doesn't know won't hurt him.'

AA Milne (1882–1956), writer: 'If you live to be a hundred, I want to live to be a hundred minus one day so I never have to live without you.'

Audrey Hepburn (1929–93), actress: 'The best thing to hold onto in life is each other.'

John Lennon (1940–80), pop star: 'Love is the flower you've got to let grow.'

Rita Rudner (b. 1953), comedienne: 'Before I met my husband, I'd never fallen in love. I'd stepped in it a few times.' Rita also said: 'I love being married. It's so great to find that one special person you want to annoy for the rest of your life.'

GK Chesterton (1874–1936), Catholic writer: 'The way to love anything is to realise that it may be lost.' And: 'Marriage is an adventure, like going to war.'

Henny Youngman (1906–98), musical comedian: 'Some people ask the secret of our long marriage. Well, we take time to go to a restaurant two times a week: a little candlelight, dinner, soft music and dancing. She goes Tuesdays, I go Fridays.' And: 'The secret of a happy marriage remains a secret.'

Lana Turner (1921–95), actress: 'A successful man is one who makes more money than his wife can spend. A successful woman is one who can find such a man.'

George Bernard Shaw (1856–1950), writer: 'Marriage is an alliance entered into by a man who can't sleep with the window shut, and a woman who can't sleep with the window open.'

GBS also said: 'When two people are under the influence of the most violent, most insane, most delusive, and most transient of passions, they are required to swear that they will remain in that excited, abnormal, and exhausting condition continuously until death do them part.'

And: 'It's a woman's business to get married as soon as possible, and a man's to keep unmarried as long as he can.'

Groucho Marx (1890–1977), comic: 'Hollywood brides keep the bouquets and throw away the grooms.' Groucho again: 'I was married by a judge. I should have asked for a jury.'

Beverley Nichols (1898–1983), playwright: 'Marriage – a book of which the first chapter is written in poetry and the remaining chapters written in prose.'

Benjamin Franklin (1706–90), Founding Father of the US: 'Keep your eyes wide open before marriage, and half-shut afterwards.'

Barbra Streisand (b. 1942), singer: 'Why does a woman work ten years to change a man, then complain he's not the man she married?'

Natalie Wood (1938–81), actress: 'The only time a woman really succeeds in changing a man is when he's a baby.'

William Goldman (b. 1931), writer: 'Mawidge [marriage] is a dweam wiffin a dweam. The dweam of wuv wapped wiffin the gweater dweam of everwasting west. Eternity is our fwiend, wemember that, and wuv wiw fowwow you fowever.'

Alfred, Lord Tennyson (1809–92), poet: ''Tis better to have loved and lost than never to have loved at all.'

Euripides (480–406 BC), tragedian: 'Love is all we have – the only way that each can help the other.'

Ovid (43 BC – AD 18), poet: 'Fortune and love favour the brave.'

Lord Byron (1788–1824), poet: 'Friendship is love without the wings.'

Ogden Nash (1902–71), poet: 'The reason for much matrimony is patrimony.' And from Nash's 'A Word to Husbands':

> To keep your marriage brimming
> With love in the marriage cup,
> Whenever you're wrong, admit it;
> Whenever you're right, shut up

...and Nash's 'I do, I will, I have':

> ...Just as I am unsure of the difference between flora and fauna and flotsam and jetsam, I am quite sure that marriage is the alliance of two people one of whom never remembers birthdays and the other never forgetsam.'

Peter de Vries (1910–93), writer: 'The bonds of matrimony are like any other bonds – they mature slowly.' And: 'The difficulty with marriage is that we fall in love with a personality, but must live with a character.'

Phyllis Diller (1917–2012), comedienne: 'Never go to bed mad. Stay up and fight.'

Jill Bennett (1931–90), actress: 'Never marry a man who hates his mother, because he'll end up hating you.'

Isadora Duncan (1877–1927), dancer: 'Any intelligent woman who reads the marriage contract, and then goes into it, deserves all the consequences.'

Ambrose Bierce (1842–1913), editor, in *The Devil's Dictionary* defines marriage thus: 'A community consisting of a master, a mistress, and two slaves, making in all two.'
And: 'Love: A temporary insanity curable by marriage.'

MM Musselman (1899–1952), writer: 'One of the best things about marriage is that it gets young people to bed at a decent hour.'

André Maurois (1885–1967), French author: 'A happy marriage is a long conversation that always seems too short.

And 'A successful marriage is an edifice that must be rebuilt every day.'

'A marriage without conflicts is almost as inconceivable as a nation without crises.

And: 'Men and women are not born inconstant: they are made so by their early amorous experiences.'

Dave Meurer (b. *c.* 1970), humorist: 'A great marriage is not when 'the perfect couple' come together, it is when an imperfect couple learns to enjoy their differences.'

Mickey Rooney (b. 1920, married 8 times), actor: 'Always get married in the morning. That way, if it doesn't work out, you haven't wasted a whole day.'

Helen Rowland (1875–1950), journalist: 'One man's folly is another man's wife.'

AP Herbert (1890–1971), novelist: 'The conception of two people living together for twenty-five years without having a cross word suggests a lack of spirit only to be admired in sheep.'

Clint Eastwood (b. 1930), actor: 'There's only one way to have a happy marriage and as soon as I learn what it is I'll get married again.'

Albert Einstein (1879–1955), physicist: 'Gravitation is not responsible for people falling in love.'

Robert Louis Stevenson (1850–94), writer: 'Marriage is like life in this – that it is a field of battle and not a bed of roses.'

Ellen Key (1849–1926), Swedish feminist: 'Love is moral even without legal marriage, but marriage is immoral without love.'

Dorothy Parker (1893–1967), satirist:

> By the time you swear you're his,
> Shivering and sighing.
> And he vows his passion is,
> Infinite, undying.
> Lady make note of this —
> One of you is lying.

Michael Winner (1935–2013), film director: 'Men are pigs, darling. I really have every sympathy for women that they actually have to choose one of these arrogant, stupid morons to settle down with and marry.'

Milton Berle (1908–2002), satirist: 'A good wife always forgives her husband when she's wrong.'

Dr Theodor Seuss (1904–91), author: 'You know you're in love when you can't fall asleep because reality is finally better than your dreams.'

Michel de Montaigne (1533–92), statesman: 'Marriage is like a cage. One sees the birds outside desperate to get in, and those inside equally desperate to get out.'

Jean Rostand (1894-1972), French biologist: 'A married couple are well-suited when both partners feel the need for a quarrel at the same time.'

Heinrich Heine (1797–1856), poet: 'Music played at weddings always reminds me of the music played for soldiers before they go into battle.'

Samuel Johnson (1709–84), dictionary compiler: 'Marriage has many pains but celibacy has no pleasures.'

Shakespeare (1564–1616) always tried to have the last word: 'Many a good hanging prevents a bad marriage.'

WEDLOCK IN LITERATURE

Many writers have put pen to parchment or paper over the centuries to comment on the state of matrimony. Here is a brief selection:

Henry Fielding (1707–54), *Tom Jones*: 'His designs were strictly honourable, as the phrase is, that is, to rob a lady of her fortune by way of marriage.'

Fielding again: 'When widows exclaim loudly against second marriage, I would always lay a wager that the man, if not the wedding day, is absolutely fixed on.'

Sydney Smith (1771–1845), essayist: 'My definition of marriage is it resembles a pair of shears, so joined that they cannot be separated; often moving in opposite directions, yet always punishing anyone who comes between them.'

JRR Tolkien (1892–1973), in a letter to his son Michael, 1941: 'Nearly all marriages, even happy ones, are mistakes; in the sense that almost certainly (in a more perfect world, or even with a little more care in this very imperfect one) both partners might be found more suitable mates. But the real soul-mate is the one you are actually married to.'

Jennifer E Smith (b. *c.* 1980), *The Statistical Probability of Love at First Sight*, 2012: 'Not everyone makes it fifty-two years, and if you do, it doesn't matter that you once stood in front of all those people and said that you would. The important part is that you had someone to stick by you all the time. Even when everything sucked.'

Charles Dickens (1812–70), *Great Expectations*: 'There can be no disparity in marriage like unsuitability of mind and purpose.'

Susan Jane Gilman (b. *c.* 1960), *Hypocrite in a Pouffy White Dress*: 'Weddings are giant Rorschach tests onto which everyone around you projects their fears, fantasies, and expectations — many of which they've been cultivating since the day you were born.'

Oscar Wilde (1854–1900), *A Woman of No Importance*:

'Twenty years of romance makes a woman look something like a ruin. Twenty years of marriage make her look something like a public building.'

'Men marry because they are tired; women because they are curious. Both are disappointed.'

'I don't see anything romantic in proposing. It is very romantic to be in love. But there is nothing romantic about a definite proposal. Why, one may be accepted. One usually is, I believe. Then the excitement is all over. The very essence of romance is uncertainty.'

And from *The Importance of Being Earnest*: 'To speak frankly, I am not in favour of long engagements. They give people the opportunity of finding out each other's character before marriage, which I think is never advisable.'

'The amount of women in London who flirt with their own husbands is perfectly scandalous. It looks so bad. It is simply washing one's clean linen in public.'

Noël Coward (1899–1973), the actor/playwright, sent a wedding telegram to Gertrude Lawrence in 1940, on her marriage to a man surnamed Aldrich (in fact, her second marriage):

> Dear Mrs. A.,
> Hooray. Hooray.
> At last you are deflowered.
> On this, as every other day
> I love you. Noël Coward.

William Shakespeare (*As You Like It*, Act 4, Scene 1):

> Men are April when they woo –
> December when they wed.
> Maids are May when they are maids…
> But the sky changed when they are wives.

To conclude, here is a line of dialogue from the scriptwriters of the American TV serial, *Law and Order* (they'd been reading their *Devil's Dictionary*), as delivered by the late and lamented Jerry Orbach:

> Love? A debilitating disease instantly cured by marriage.

JANE AUSTEN'S ERA
(1775–1817)

In Britain, from the beginning of the Hanoverian era, marriage was viewed as a salvation for families with a large brood of daughters.

'Happiness in marriage is entirely a matter of chance.'

From Jane Austen's
Pride and Prejudice – Chapter 6

This is the underlying theme of much of Jane Austen's work, and accounts for what it is in her novels that seems to pluck at our heartstrings through the generations. The opening line of *Pride and Prejudice*:

'It is a truth, universally acknowledged, that a single man in possession of a good fortune, must be in want of a wife.'

Women contemporaneous with Jane Austen regarded marriage as the ultimate goal in life. But Jane, through Elizabeth in *Pride and Prejudice*, displays a more independent minded spirit.

Elizabeth: 'I am determined that nothing but the deepest love could ever induce me into matrimony.'

She follows through in melancholy muse:

'So... I shall end an old maid, and teach your ten children to embroider cushions...'

In *Pride and Prejudice*, the Bennet family, middle-class but not overly well off, are blessed with five daughters. For the girls to avert the fate of facing impoverished spinsterhood, it is essential that husbands should be found for them.

We witness Mrs. Bennet's growing pleasure as, one by one, her daughters find men to take them on. Her youngest daughter, Lydia, is the first to go.

'Well! I am so happy. In a short time I shall have a daughter married, Mrs. Wickham! How well it sounds. And she was only sixteen last June.'

In *Emma* Austen writes: 'It is always incomprehensible to a man that a woman should ever refuse an offer of marriage.'

And in *Northanger Abbey*:

> And such is your definition of matrimony and dancing. Taken in that light, certainly their resemblance is not striking; but I think I could place them in such a view. You will allow that in both man has the advantage of choice, woman only the power of refusal; that in both it is an engagement between man and woman, formed for the advantage of each; and that when once entered into, they belong exclusively to each other till the moment of its dissolution; that it is their duty each to endeavor to give the other no cause for wishing that he or she had bestowed themselves elsewhere, and their best interest to keep their own imaginations from wandering towards the perfections of their neighbours, or fancying that they should have been better off with any one else.

It is one of life's little ironies that for all the wedding bells that rang out for Jane Austen's heroines, they did not chime for the author herself. Regarding her flirtatious association with Tom Lefroy, Jane wrote in a letter:

> At length the day has come on which I am to flirt my last with Mr Tom Lefroy, and when you receive this it will be over. My tears flow as I write at the melancholy idea!

She had turned down several proposals of marriage and broken off at least two engagements. In later life she claimed to be relieved at having avoided the pitfalls of matrimony. Until the modern era, giving birth was a precarious business, and that might have been in Jane's mind when she wrote, 'all that business of Mothering!'

Perhaps we should be grateful that Jane Austen sacrificed a life of married domesticity for the freedom to write.

Epilogue & Appendices

Epilogue

I was about 40 by the time I started earning sufficient money to indulge in the odd luxury. It was then that I bought the *Encyclopædia Britannica*, 17th Edition, in 32 volumes including the Index books. As I type these words, Volume 7 rests under my left elbow. The wonderful Encyclopædia (how I love that ligature) has served as my final arbiter when I've had a choice of contradictory facts from which to select the most likely truth. There are bound to be readers who know details of various traditions and superstitions that have not been mentioned in this book. For any omissions, I apologise. For any revelations, I wag my tail.

For all the Lies and the Damned Lies and the Statistics quoted in this book, I gratefully acknowledge HM Government's official website. It should be borne in mind that statistics are ephemeral and change before our very eyes. I don't claim to be alone in ploughing this fertile ground. Other writers have toiled in adjacent furrows. Some have come up with wheat and others with sweetcorn. I hope that my work will harvest a cornucopia of delights. I certainly enjoyed planting the seeds.My other chief reference has been my wife Barbara who knows something about marriage. We tied the knot 51 years ago at Burnt Oak Register Office. I owned one dark blue suit. Now, I possess two. And we have grandchildren. So she has proved a positive influence on me. What's more, she has patiently read the early drafts of this book, making a raft of helpful suggestions.I owe some of the more bizarre historical references to another book called *The Book of Royal Useless Information* that I wrote with the late Noel Botham. It too is published by John Blake Ltd.

BRUCE MONTAGUE

Appendix I

Extract from the Decree of the Council of Trent (November 1563)

In 1563, at the 24th Session of the Council of Trent in its Decree on the Reformation of Marriage, under the sovereign Pontiff, Pius IV, it was stated categorically:

'Those who shall attempt to contract marriage otherwise than in the presence of the parish priest, or of some other priest by permission of the said parish priest, or of the Ordinary, and in the presence of two or three witnesses; the holy Synod renders such wholly incapable of thus contracting and declares such contracts invalid and null, as by the present decree It invalidates and annuls them.

Moreover It enjoins, that the parish priest, or any other priest, who shall have been present at any such contract with a less number of witnesses (than as aforesaid); as also the witnesses who have been present thereat without the parish priest, or some other priest; and also the contracting parties themselves; shall be severely punished, at the discretion of the Ordinary. Furthermore, the same holy Synod exhorts the bridegroom and bride not to live together in the same house until they have received the sacerdotal benediction, which is to be given in the church; and It ordains that the benediction shall be given by their own parish priest, and that permission to give the aforesaid benediction cannot be granted by any other than the parish priest himself, or the Ordinary; any custom, even though immemorial, which ought rather to be called a corruption, or any privilege to the contrary, notwithstanding. And if any parish priest, or any other priest, whether Regular or Secular, shall presume to unite in marriage the betrothed of another parish, or to bless them when married, without the permission of their parish priest, he shall – even though he may plead that he is allowed to do this by a privilege, or an immemorial custom – remain ipso jure suspended, until absolved by the Ordinary of that parish priest who ought to have been present at the marriage, or from whom the benediction ought to have been received.

Appendix 2

The Solemnisation of Marriage

Extract from The Directory for Public Worship *(1645)*

That ALTHOUGH marriage be no sacrament, nor peculiar to the church of God, but common to mankind, and of publick interest in every commonwealth; yet, because such as marry are to marry in the Lord, and have special need of instruction, direction, and exhortation, from the word of God, at their entering into such a new condition, and of the blessing of God upon them therein, we judge it expedient that marriage be solemnised by a lawful minister of the word, that he may accordingly counsel them, and pray for a blessing upon them.

Marriage is to be betwixt one man and one woman only; and they such as are not within the degrees of consanguinity or affinity prohibited by the word of God; and the parties are to be of years of discretion, fit to make their own choice, or, upon good grounds, to give their mutual consent.

Before the solemnising of marriage between any persons, the purpose of marriage shall be published by the minister three several sabbath-days, in the congregation, at the place or places of their most usual and constant abode, respectively. And of this publication the minister who is to join them in marriage shall have sufficient testimony, before he proceed to solemnise the marriage.

Before that publication of such their purpose, (if the parties be under age,) the consent of the parents, or others under whose power they are, (in case the parents be dead,) is to be made known to the church officers of that congregation, to be recorded.

The like is to be observed in the proceedings of all others, although of age, whose parents are living, for their first marriage.

And, in after marriages of either of those parties, they shall be exhorted not to contract marriage without first acquainting their parents with it, (if with conveniency it may be done,) endeavouring to obtain their consent.

Parents ought not to force their children to marry without their free consent, nor deny their own consent without just cause.

After the purpose or contract of marriage hath been thus published, the marriage is not to be long deferred. Therefore the minister, having had convenient warning, and nothing being objected to hinder it, is publickly to solemnise it in the place appointed by authority for publick worship, before a competent number of credible witnesses, at some convenient hour of the day, at any time of the year, except on a day of publick humiliation. And we advise that it be not on the Lord's day.

And because all relations are sanctified by the word and prayer, the minister is to pray for a blessing upon them, to this effect:

> 'Acknowledging our sins, whereby we have made ourselves less than the least of all the mercies of God, and provoked him to embitter all our comforts; earnestly, in the name of Christ, to entreat the Lord (whose presence and favour is the happiness of every condition, and sweetens every relation) to be their

portion, and to own and accept them in Christ, who are now to be joined in the honourable estate of marriage, the covenant of their God: and that, as he hath brought them together by his providence, he would sanctify them by his Spirit, giving them a new frame of heart fit for their new estate; enriching them with all graces whereby they may perform the duties, enjoy the comforts, undergo the cares, and resist the temptations which accompany that condition, as becometh Christians.'

The prayer being ended, it is convenient that the minister do briefly declare unto them, out of the scripture,

'The institution, use, and ends of marriage, with the conjugal duties, which, in all faithfulness, they are to perform each to other; exhorting them to study the holy word of God, that they may learn to live by faith, and to be content in the midst of all marriage cares and troubles, sanctifying God's name, in a thankful, sober, and holy use of all conjugal comforts; praying much with and for one another; watching over and provoking each other to love and good works; and to live together as the heirs of the grace of life.'

After solemn charging of the persons to be married, before the great God, who searcheth all hearts, and to whom they must give a strict account at the last day, that if either of them know any cause, by precontract or otherwise, why they may not lawfully proceed to marriage, that they now discover it; the minister (if no impediment be acknowledged) shall cause first the man to take the woman by the right hand, saying these words:

> *I (NAME) do take thee (NAME) to be my married wife, and do, in the presence of God, and before this congregation, promise and covenant to be a loving and faithful husband unto thee, until God shall separate us by death.*

Then the woman shall take the man by the right hand, and say these words:

> *I (NAME) do take thee (NAME) to be my married husband, and I do, in the presence of God, and before this congregation, promise and covenant to be a loving, faithful, and obedient wife unto thee, until God shall separate us by death.*

Then, without any further ceremony, the minister shall, in the face of the congregation, pronounce them to be husband and wife, according to God's ordinance; and so conclude the action with prayer to this effect:

> 'That the Lord would be pleased to accompany his own ordinance with his blessing, beseeching him to enrich the persons now married, as with other pledges of his love, so particularly with the comforts and fruits of marriage, to the praise of his abundant mercy, in and through Christ Jesus.'

A register is to be carefully kept, wherein the names of the parties so married, with the time of their marriage, are forthwith to be fairly recorded in a book provided for that purpose, for the perusal of all whom it may concern.

Appendix 3

From the Book of Judges (21:19–23; King James Version)

Then they said, Behold, there is a feast of the Lord in Shiloh... Therefore they commanded the children of Benjamin, saying, Go and lie in wait in the vineyards. And see, and, behold, if the daughters of Shiloh come out to dance in dances, then come ye out of the vineyards, and catch you every man his wife of the daughters of Shiloh, and go to the land of Benjamin. And it shall be, when their fathers or their brethren come unto us to complain, that we will say unto them, Be favourable unto them for our sakes: because we reserved not to each man his wife in the war: for ye did not give unto them at this time, that ye should be guilty. And the children of Benjamin did so, and took them wives, according to their number, of them that danced, whom they caught: and they went and returned unto their inheritance, and repaired the cities, and dwelt in them.